SEXPIONAGE

For the KGB, sexpionage is a subject neither for humour nor ridicule. It is a serious and complex technique of subversion which occupies the time of thousands of staff officers, technicians, bed partners and surveillance experts. They maintain special apartments in Moscow where entrapments can be carried out, have bedrooms fitted with photographic and electronic equipment in major hotels all over the Soviet Union, and run special sex schools where male and female bed partners are trained. Clearly the KGB has invested an enormous amount of money and time in the sexpionage industry. Has it paid off?

Sexpionage

The Exploitation of Sex by Soviet Intelligence

David Lewis

Heinrich Hanau Publications London

First published in Great Britain by
Heinrich Hanau Publications Ltd 1976
This edition published 1977

Copyright © David Lewis 1976

All rights reserved

Printed in Great Britain by
Cox & Wyman Ltd, London, Reading and Fakenham

ISBN 0426 08723 2

To Peter

How cheerfully he seems to grin,
 How neatly spreads his claws,
And welcomes little fishes in
 With gently smiling jaws!

—Lewis Carroll, *Alice's Adventures in Wonderland*

Contents

Glossary xiii

Introduction 3

1 Their Trade Is Treachery 9

2 The Spider of Dzerzhinsky Square 23

3 Secrets of the Sex Schools 33

4 Confessions of a Swallow 46

5 Birds of Prey 61

6 Ravens 76

7 Brothels and Blue Films 92

8 Assault on NATO 101

9 On Her Majesty's Sexual Service 122

10 Invasion of the Bedrooms 138

11 Safeguarding Our Secrets 150

Commentary on Sources 155

Bibliography 159

Index 163

Glossary

BfV

Bundesamt für Verfassungsschutz (Federal Office for the Protection of the Constitution). West German counterintelligence.

BND

Bundesnachrichtendienst (German Federal Intelligence Service). Formerly the Bureau Gehlen. Set up by the Americans and heavily infiltrated by the CIA.

CIA

Central Intelligence Agency. United States foreign intelligence organization.

Dead drop

Also known as a dead-letter box. A location where agents can safely leave messages for collection.

Disinformation

The planting of false information in the press, radio, and TV and the production of "sponsored" books by security-service writers, etc. Used by all the major services.

DST

Direction de la Sécurité du Territoire. French agency charged with internal security.

ELINT

Electronic intelligence. The gathering of intelligence by means of spyplanes, satellites, video monitors, and other technological means.

End-of-the-line agent

CIA jargon for a man or woman, usually a foreign national, who carries out an actual espionage operation, either providing direct information or services such as transport, safe apartments for meetings, etc. These agents work under case officers who are career CIA men.

GLOSSARY

Executive action
A CIA euphemism for having somebody killed.

FBI
Federal Bureau of Investigation. United States internal security agency

GRU
Glavnoye Razvedyvatelnoye Upravleniye. Soviet military intelligence.

Illegal
An undercover spy. Will be arrested and jailed if caught.

KGB
Komitet Gosudarstvennoy Bezopasnosti (Committee of State Security). The Soviet Union's secret service.

Legal
Spy, or spy master, using diplomatic cover for espionage activity. If caught, can only be deported.

MAD
Militärischer Abschirmdienst. Military counterintelligence in West Germany

MfS
Ministerium für Staatssicherheit. Ministry for State Security in East Germany

NSA
The National Security Agency. America's code-breaking and -making service. In terms of intelligence gathering, it is more important than the CIA.

OSS
Office of Strategic Services. The American World War II intelligence and sabotage organization. Precursor to the CIA.

Positive vetting
A security clearance classification indicating that the subject has been checked and found to be reliable.

Raven
A male KGB prostitute spy.

GLOSSARY

SDECE

Service de Documentation Extérieure et de Contre-Espionnage. The French secret service. Headquarters located in the north of Paris.

Security Service

British counterintelligence service responsible for security within the United Kingdom. Sometimes referred to as MI-5, its World War II name.

SHAPE

Supreme Headquarters Allied Powers Europe. Military command of the North Atlantic Treaty Organization. Since 1967 SHAPE has been located outside Mons, in Belgium, some forty miles from Brussels.

SIS

Secret Intelligence Service. British organization for espionage outside the United Kingdom. Known during World War II as MI-6.

STB

Statni Tajna Bezpecnost. The Czech intelligence service. Like the services of all Soviet bloc countries, it works closely with the KGB. Although technically the First Section of the Intelligence Directorate of the Ministry of the Interior, it is usually known as the State Secret Security of STB.

Swallow

A female KGB prostitute spy.

Wet work

Any operation which involves the shedding of blood (wet stuff). A CIA euphemism.

Acknowledgments

Many of those friends and contacts who helped me arrange interviews, set up meetings or simply provided the odd pieces of information which helped to complete part of a frequently bewildering jigsaw puzzle would be horrified to see their names here. This anonymity was desired most strongly by the women who talked about their experiences as sexpionage "swallows." Having escaped from the nightmare, it was frequently painful for them to relive their memories through an interview. Their one desire was to slip back into the normal world. To all of them, however, my thanks. I would also like to thank Hans Tasiemka, of London, for access to his unique archives and the staff of the London Library for their unfailing courtesy and help. My thanks too for the help given by my research assistants in Germany, who have also asked not to be named, for sound reasons. Finally, my thanks to Dr. Robert Sharpe, at the Center for Applied Behavioral Sciences, for helping me to understand the psycho-sexual background of the distasteful but fascinating world of sexpionage.

Sexpionage

Introduction

Sex and spying have always been intimately related. Not only are prostitution and espionage two of the oldest professions, they are also among mankind's most secret and covertly influential activities. This ancient alliance between the desires of the body and the schemings of the intellect has probably played a more significant role in shaping history than the endeavors of generations of generals and politicans.

The traditional task of the sex spy, in fact as well as in fiction, was to seduce an infatuated lover into revealing secrets. To use the double bed as a passport to indiscreet pillow-talk is a technique of Biblical antiquity. In the tenth century B.C., the first recorded sex spy, Delilah, used her charms to destroy the Danite hero Samson. In the twentieth century, Nazi prostitute spies used their bodies in the same way to tease indiscretions from clients in Gestapo-run brothels.

Since 1945, however, not only has this ancient technique become part of far more complex entrapment operations, but the end to which it is used has largely changed. Instead of a means of gleaning secrets, sex is now used as a method of subverting the loyalty of the individual. Painstakingly constructed sex snares are devised to produce evidence which can then be used as blackmail evidence to force the victims to work against their country's best interests. Such entrapments are frequent in Soviet bloc countries. They are often complicated and costly, involving scores of skilled operatives and the most advanced electronic and photographic equipment. They are always carried out with a cynical disregard for the feelings of those involved. Usually they are successful. This modern, technologically sophisticated use of an age-old espionage technique has been called "sexpionage."

Sexpionage operations are carried out on a world-wide basis and involve a multimillion dollar annual expenditure. Since the last world war the technique has enabled the Soviet Union to achieve several major espionage coups against the West. Yet most of the accomplishments of sexpionage, as well as its recruitment and training techniques and operational procedures, have remained cloaked with secrecy.

To place sexpionage in its historic perspective it will be useful to briefly review the development of intelligence gathering during the last 400 years.

At the turn of this century espionage techniques had changed little since the days of Sir Francis Walsingham, the sixteenth-century father of modern spying. As spy master to Queen Elizabeth I, Walsingham established the foundations on which subsequent secret services were to be built. His elaborate and well-financed intelligence service controlled hundreds of agents in Britain and abroad. It was charged with the dual task of safeguarding the throne from domestic intrigue and the country from invasion. At home his spies kept a close watch on plots centered around Mary, Queen of Scots. In Europe his agents, many of them impecunious young Englishmen studying abroad, investigated the territorial ambitions of monarchs like Philip of Spain. It was through Walsingham's efforts that Britain got useful early warning of the Spanish armada.

Three hundred years later British military intelligence sent Sir Robert Baden-Powell, founder of the Boy Scout movement, into the Austro-Hungarian Empire on a mission which Sir Francis would have applauded. His assignment was to make drawings of military fortifications. His ploy was to act the part of a short-sighted naturalist. This enabled him to penetrate restricted areas on the pretext of hunting for butterflies. He disguised his secret sketches in the design and shading of natural history drawings. It was spying in the best of cloak-and-dagger traditions.

As late as 1915, war was regarded by many people in Britain as a kind of game to be played by gentlemen according to unwritten but clearly understood codes of honor. In 1914, for example, the British War Office turned down the idea of using trench periscopes for surveying the enemy battlefronts. It would have saved hundreds of lives but the British high command decided that "it is contrary to the traditions of the officer to seek information about the enemy from a place of safety by means of a mechanical contrivance."

In espionage, as in war, the spy masters preferred to behave in what they considered an honorable manner. It was an attitude of mind perfectly illustrated by the story of the United States Secretary of State, Henry L. Stimson and the code crackers. In the years following World War I, American military intelligence operated a very secret and highly effec-

INTRODUCTION

tive cryptologic section known as the "Black Chamber." In 1920 this department had succeeded in breaking the Japanese diplomatic cipher, a major espionage achievement. However, in 1929, Henry Stimson effectively closed down the department with the terse comment that "gentlemen do not read each other's mail."

The Cold War and the nuclear arms race have buried such questionable gallantry for all time. Today the work of the major espionage organizations has expanded to include a wide variety of activities other than intelligence gathering. These have been suitably described as "dirty tricks."

Dirty tricks include disinformation, the spreading of false information to confuse people; assassinations; the infiltration of an opponent's institutions; and the "destabilization" of unfriendly governments—any activity, in fact, which policy makers deem useful.

As the workload has expanded, so has the number of potential targets and today the term "opponent" is an all-embracing one. In Britain, for example, the United States Central Intelligence Agency (CIA) and the United Kingdom's Secret Intelligence Service (SIS) work closely on many operations. But, at the same time, the CIA actively spies on the British and attempts to infiltrate their major institutions. Where possible the SIS responds in kind. In some areas, for example the Middle East, the Soviet Union's Committee of State Security (KGB) and the CIA have been known to work together at a field level against a third party. In Britain official policy operates against the South African government, but this does not prevent the SIS working with the South African Bureau of State Security when the need arises.

The expansion of power, influence, and wealth of these agencies has occurred alongside a decline in the more traditional techniques and a rise in the importance of ELINT or electronic intelligence-gathering. During the 1973 Middle East War, for example, both the United States and Soviet Union used spy satellites as a primary source of information. These are orbiting the earth today, keeping photographic and electronic surveillance observation over every significant square mile of the earth's surface.

The United States launches reconnaissance and surveillance satellites regularly from Vandenberg Air Force Base, California. The Soviet Union puts its spies into orbit from Kapustin Yar, Tyuratam, and Plesetsk. One type of US satellite, known as the ferret or COMLINT (communications intelligence), is designed to intercept and record foreign communications. These satellites have polar or near-polar orbits between 300 and 500 miles above the earth. As they pass over friendly territory the recordings are transmitted to a tracking station and the tapes used again. Satellites of this type have been used to intercept car telephone calls made by the Soviet leaders and to eavesdrop on the messages passing between tank commanders on exercises in the Urals. Other satellites have infrared detectors which measure changes in ground temperature and are able to pinpoint ballistic-missile silos. They can also be used to locate submerged submarines.

Photographic reconnaissance satellites are equipped with two types of camera, one to provide a general view of the terrain, another to take high resolution close-ups. The 72″ lens on the SAMOS series of satellites is said to be capable of picking out a small car from 200 miles in space, while the claim for the 96″ lens of the "Big Bird" satellite is even more remarkable. One report says it can record the details of a newspaper headline from the same altitude. Apart from these general surveillance satellites, there are a number of specialist spies in orbit. As long ago as 1962 the United States launched satellites capable of detecting the products of nuclear fission. Today two satellites, 50,000 miles apart, can monitor all above-ground nuclear explosions and even be used to predict such a test long before it happens. In May 1965, for example, the public learned that the Chinese had exploded a nuclear device in the atmosphere. The announcement came as no surprise to officials of the US Atomic Energy Commission. Months before the test their satellites had alerted them to the fact that a plutonium reactor was operating at Paotow in Inner Mongolia. This indicated that the raw material for such a bomb was under production. The satellites not only located the plants in the remote and heavily guarded region, but even identified the number of reactors within the complex. It was an espionage coup which no human agent could have ever achieved.

In 1964 the KGB may have been slightly embarrassed by the massive publicity given to the discovery of forty bulky microphones buried in the walls of the American Embassy in Moscow. Today such devices are regarded as antique. Electronic "chip" technology enables transmitters to be built which can be fitted inside a tooth, a fake nipple, or even strapped to the back of a fly. The CIA has designed a laser listening device which enables a room to be bugged—at least in theory—without an agent ever going near it. A laser beam is bounced off a window, or some object like a map or chart hanging in the room. Vibrations caused by

INTRODUCTION

sound waves interfere with the beam and create fluctuations in the returned signal which can be converted back into speech patterns. In practice this device has proved less reliable than was expected, although it does work well in Africa for some unknown reason.

Where have these technological advances left the traditional spy? Has the cloak been exchanged for a laboratory coat and the dagger for a slide rule?

The answer, as far as routine intelligence gathering is concerned, must be a qualified yes. During World War II the Allies managed a fairly deep penetration of the German High Command. No similar feat has been achieved, as far as is known, by the CIA where either the Russians or Chinese are concerned. Nor have those two peoples, working under easier conditions in the open society of the United States, achieved much greater success. Most of the West's non-ELINT information has come from defectors and the occasional traitor like Colonel Oleg Penkovsky.

This does not mean that spies, the foot soldiers of the espionage war, have been pensioned off completely. There are still many areas of the world—Germany and Italy stand out as the main European territories—where they can render valuable services in the traditional infiltration roles. As far as dirty tricks, sabotage, disinformation, subversion, and sexpionage are concerned, spies are, of course, essential. Improved technology may make the setting up of entrapments easier and more certain; improved recording techniques will ensure that the most dim and distant image of copulation can be filmed in sharp focus and with perfect exposure. But no piece of gadgetry, however brilliantly designed, can yet replace the basic element of all sexpionage operations—the warm and willing body of a fellow human being.

1

Their Trade Is Treachery

Since 1945 the KGB has used sexpionage to obtain a wide range of top-secret military, political, industrial, and economic information from the West. They have used sexpionage to pre-empt counterintelligence coups against their agents, to disgrace and discredit political opponents of the Soviet Union abroad, and to deeply infiltrate the North Atlantic Treaty Organization (NATO).

Although many countries make use of sexpionage, no secret service has invested as much time, effort, and thought in the technique as the KGB. By using specially trained prostitute spies—male and female—and combining their skills with the latest technological advances in electronics, photography and computer programing, the Soviet secret service has achieved the most refined form of sexpionage possible. On the age-old foundation of sexual attraction they have created an elaborate industry of intelligence gathering and subversion which, in many ways, surpasses all the complicated electronic gadgetry of America's espionage establishment.

The Earl of Chesterfield dismissed sexual intercourse with the comment that the pleasure was momentary, the position ridiculous, and the expense damnable. Many victims of sexpionage entrapments would echo the nineteenth-century aristocrat's sentiments. When the KGB writes out a bill for the liaisons which it has manipulated, the charges may include broken careers, shattered marriages, years of imprisonment and, sometimes, death.

To illustrate how the various elements of a sexpionage operation are slotted together, let's follow a case history drawn from the files of a European intelligence service. Since to identify the victim could still damage his career and private life, his name and some other details have been altered.

Phillippe Latour was forty-two years old when he paid his first visit to Russia in the late sixties. An electronics engineer, he worked for a company engaged in the development of missile guidance systems for the French government. As an authority in his specialized field he had traveled to Warsaw Pact countries on a number of occasions to attend conferences and address scientific gatherings. In his spare time Monsieur Latour was a keen amateur historian and he had for several years been eager to visit Moscow and Leningrad to see the museum and study at first hand the many fine pre-Revolution buildings.

Phillippe finally realized his ambition one August when he persuaded his wife to take their three children to spend the month on the Mediterranean while he took two weeks off to explore the Soviet Union. A few days after settling his family into their villa at Eze-sur-Mer, Phillippe flew to Moscow and checked into the Metropole Hotel on Ploshchad Sverdlova. He spent the next six days sight-seeing, blissfully unaware of the fact that only a stone's throw from his hotel room, behind the gray walls of the KGB's headquarters at 2 Dzerzhinsky Square, the details of an elaborate entrapment were being finalized.

The entrapment had been decided on soon after his visa application had arrived as a matter of routine, along with hundreds of others, in the offices of the KGB's Second Chief Directorate. The information provided on Latour's form was fed into a computer and, a few moments later, the teleprinter was clattering out a highly detailed biography, the result of many previous hours' research and surveillance by KGB agents. The dossier which arrived on the desk of a staff officer in the Second Section of the Second Chief Directorate contained the information under the following headings:

BASIC DATA: Present position and previous work. Prospects of remaining in present employment. Prospects of promotion. Date joined present employment. Personal attitudes towards work and employment. Details of classified work undertaken.

BIOGRAPHICAL DATA: Age, parents, family conditions. Education; principal specialization; technical or other knowledge. Attitude towards politics. Party affiliations; opinions on state administration. Financial position. Attitude towards USSR and Soviet politics. Subject's view of prosperity of his/her country.

PERSONAL POSITIVE AND NEGATIVE CHARACTERISTICS: Inclination to drink. Women friends. Family relationships. Love of luxury. Interest in solitude. Sexual deviations and perversions. Influence of wife/husband on actions. Independence of decision making. Friends and associates at work.

In the case of Phillippe Latour, the basic data section informed the staff officer that Latour had achieved a senior position in his company through hard work and ability, a useful combination catalyzed by an even more useful marriage to the daughter of a senior government official. It also noted that Latour was careful, conscientious, and very ambitious. The biographical section revealed that he was generally apolitical as far as party politics were concerned, but conservative by nature. His financial position was sound, largely thanks to his wife's money, and his attitude towards the USSR and Communism was one of distrust and distaste. The final section of his record showed that like most men he had a weakness for good food and drink and an eye for a pretty woman.

Latour's dossier had been started by the KGB early in his career when he first rose to prominence in scientific circles. The file was partly compiled from "white sources"—that is, non-classified material published in newspapers, biographical reference books, and scientific magazines—and partly from KGB undercover spies, known as "illegals," making enquiries among his friends and neighbors, possibly with the excuse of assessing his credit worthiness for a loan. Over the years the specks of information had been accumulated and collated in the central index at "the Center," as the KGB's Moscow headquarters are called. Now the result of all this diligent effort was set down in neatly typed lines on a sheet of flimsy computer print-out paper. Latour's unexpected visit to the Soviet Union offered the chance of putting the work to positive use. It was an opportunity not to be missed.

With his sight-seeing in Moscow completed, Phillippe traveled to Leningrad. He had been booked, by Intourist, into the comfortable Baltic Hotel on Nevsky Prospekt, but when he gave his name to the desk clerk the response was unexpected. After running his finger down a list of reservations the man shook his head.

"There is no such booking," he told Latour. Latour protested angrily and a manager arrived. Phone calls were made to the Intourist office. Finally the official apologized to Latour. There had been an inexcusable mix-up, but there was no need to worry. They could not provide him with a single room, but a suite on the third floor was available. They would be delighted to let him have it at no extra cost by way of apology for the error.

The rooms were spacious and comfortably furnished, with a lounge opening off the bedroom, and an elegant private bathroom. Ten minutes later there was a knock on the door and a waiter appeared with half a bottle of vodka and a dish of caviar, courtesy gifts, he explained, from Intourist.

Phillippe Latour then set off for an afternoon's sight-seeing. He visited the Winter Palace and the Old Hermitage, then crossed the River Neva to photograph the Peter and Paul Fortress from Revolution Square. All this time, quite unknown to him, Latour was being subjected to continuous observation by a small army of KGB agents. The time he returned to his hotel was noted. When, two hours later, washed and rested, he strolled out again onto Nevsky Prospekt in search of an evening meal, a skilled surveillance expert detached himself from a shop doorway and sauntered casually after him. At 25 Nevsky Prospekt, Latour stopped outside the Kavasky, a popular Caucasian restaurant, and then went inside. While one agent followed him into the Kavasky and kept watch from a nearby table, another radioed this information from an unmarked car parked in the street. It was time to press the button and set in motion the machinery of entrapment.

Ten minutes later, a slender, well-dressed and very attractive blonde came into the Kavasky and glanced around uncertainly. Seeing an empty chair at Latour's table she made her way across the room and asked in Russian if she might join him. *"Ya ne govoryu po-russki,"* said Phillippe hesitantly, trying out one of his few Russian phrases. To his surprise the woman smiled delightedly and then said in faultless French, "You come from France I think, from your accent. My name is Tania Salakov and I am a language teacher. I enjoy talking to foreigners. May I join you?"

Latour found Tania a delightful companion. When the meal was over they walked together along the Prospekt admiring the book and art shops, and the displays of hand-woven carpets and handicrafts. They finally parted outside his hotel, having made a firm date for the following afternoon.

For the next two days Tania was Phillippe's escort and guide. They visited the Czar's Summer Palace, the Stroganov Palace and the Kazan Cathedral. On his fourth evening in Leningrad Tania took Phillippe for an after-dinner stroll along an embankment on the Moika River.

"You know, my life is not easy," she confided, as they watched the lights of the city reflected in the still, dark waters. "My husband is in the army and I seldom see him."

They stopped walking and Philippe took her in his arms. "For any woman to be neglected is a crime," he told her gallantly, "but for one so beautiful such neglect is worse than a crime, it is a mistake! But perhaps a mistake which we can remedy?"

She returned his light, tentative embrace with a warm kiss.

"We must go to your hotel," she told him. "It is not safe at my apartment; the neighbors would be sure to notice us and my husband is very jealous. If he found out. . . ."

"What about the receptionist?" Phillippe asked nervously. He too was anxious to avoid a scene or any scandal.

"In this country we mind our business about such matters," Tania said quietly.

Hand in hand, they walked back to his hotel. To Latour's relief Tania seemed to have been right about the receptionist. The *dezhurnaya* woman on duty merely nodded politely. Outside in his car a KGB surveillance agent radioed to headquarters. The "swallow," as KGB female prostitutes are called, had gone up to the target's room. The final stage of the entrapment had been reached.

When they got to the bedroom, Phillippe, feeling extremely self-conscious and unromantic, took one or two precautions. He still had a lurking doubt that the whole liaison might be a KGB trap. He knew from firsthand experience that his work on classified missile research had made him of interest to the Russians. Eighteen months earlier, while attending a conference in Warsaw, an approach had been made in a bar. A stranger with good technical knowledge had engaged him in conversation and then plied him with strong Polish vodka. Gradually the conversation turned to the high cost of living in the West, and hints had been dropped that the Polish government would pay handsomely for any information which Monsieur Latour could put their way. That tactic having failed, his companion began to describe the sufferings inflicted on his country by the Nazis during the war. Phillippe, who had fought in the Resistance, listened sympathetically. But when the conversation was again brought around to the subject of classified military information and the need for a united front against Fascist Germany in peace as in war, he made a curt excuse and left.

With this encounter in mind Phillippe now not only locked the bedroom door but wedged a chair under the handle to prevent their lovemaking from being interrupted. He then crossed the room and drew the heavy curtains to prevent any pictures being taken from the balcony. Meanwhile Tania had let her black satin dress slide to the floor to reveal a black lace brassière and lace-trimmed panties, underwear which, Phillippe decided, owed more to a Paris fashion house than the utilitarian racks of a GUM department store. Tania slid off her stockings and unfastened her garter belt.

With memories of *From Russia With Love*, Phillippe glanced anxiously at the large mirror facing the bed. It was screwed into a thin wall separating the bedroom from the lounge, and there seemed no possibility of a film camera being hidden behind it.

"Please hurry, Phillippe darling," whispered Tania, naked now, curled up on the coverlet. "I have to be at work early in the morning." However, before he removed any of his clothes or went near the bed, he switched off the light, taking what he believed to be a final precaution. The room was now in almost complete darkness; only a faint trace of yellow light filtered in through a ventilation grille between the bedroom and the corridor. An enthusiastic amateur photographer, Phillipe knew that no film made would be sensitive enough to work in that light. He quickly took off his clothes and a few moments later all traces of fear that he might be compromised vanished in the delights of love-making.

When they had finished, Tania switched on the bedside light, dressed quickly, and kissed Phillippe lightly on the forehead. "I will try and meet you tomorrow evening," she told him. "You are a wonderful lover. *Bon soir.*"

Latour never saw the woman again. The following afternoon he was requested to see the manager. In his office he found two plain-clothed KGB men. One introduced himself as a colonel, produced an envelope, and invited Latour to examine its contents.

A dozen eight-by-ten glossy photographs spilled onto the desk top. Every aspect of Latour's previous night's love-making lay before him in cold, clinical detail. His first reaction was one of horrified disbelief. He had been certain that it had been technically impossible for any photographs to be taken. Yet the awful contradiction of this belief lay on the desk before him.

Chapter ten will examine in detail the latest photographic and electronic equipment used in entrapments. In brief, the photographs of Phillippe and Tania had been taken by using a permanent photographic installation in the hotel suite. This accounted for the supposed "reservation error" which made sure that the Frenchman was directed into a bugged room. The pictures had been taken not by an ordinary camera, but by a miniature television camera built into a wall near the bed. The lens shot through a one-inch diameter opening which was concealed, when not in use, by a plaster molding. When pictures needed to be taken, the molding would automatically open. In place of a normal lens, the camera was fitted with a brightness-intensifying unit capable of increasing available light up to 150,000 times. Moonlight, even moderate starlight, would have provided enough illumination to obtain high-quality pictures. With the curtains drawn, the light entering the room via the ventilation grille had proved quite adequate. The TV pictures went by wire to a room on the ground floor where a KGB agent was able to monitor a number of similarly bugged bedrooms. The agent watched Phillippe and Tania making love through an optical device which enabled him to observe the television monitor and at the same time snap pictures from the TV screen with a still camera loaded with a fine-grain emulsion film. If the pictures had been of poor quality, then undoubtedly Tania would have kept her next appointment to give the camera another chance. As it was, her part in the entrapment was over. The bait had been taken and now the KGB officers had arrived to present Phillippe Latour with the bill, information on the homing heads of air-to-air missiles. Despite their threats of blackmail, Latour declined to provide it. He was taken from the hotel and flown, under escort, to Moscow. His protests were ignored, as were his demands to see the French ambassador.

The woman he had seduced was the wife of a senior Soviet army officer, he was told by the colonel, and obviously Latour had been sent as a spy to extract information from her. Should they decide to charge Latour, the colonel could guarantee he would be found guilty and sentenced to many years in prison.

After three days' isolation in the Lubyanka prison, Phillippe Latour's nerve snapped. He agreed to give his interrogators the information they demanded. Although the information was classified, he was certain it was not so secret that it would seriously harm his country's interests; and besides, he argued with himself, from the tidbits gleaned during questioning he was fairly certain that the Russians already knew the most important facts about the anti-jamming system.

"They were very specific in the kind of information they demanded," he told French counterintelligence officers later. "Clearly they had an excellent insight into this research."

He gave them everything required and was rewarded with the negatives and prints of the compromising photographs. What he had failed to realize was that the Russians had also video-taped the TV pictures, so that they could reproduce the blackmail material at will. However, they now had no further need of sexpionage. Latour, by disclosing secret information, had committed an act of treason for which he was likely to be jailed by the French. The KGB had a tape recording of his verbal admissions, photographs of him making the drawings they had demanded, and an explanation of the electronic circuitry in his own handwriting—more than sufficient evidence to convince a French court of the scientist's treachery. It was this lever to which the KGB now applied pressure in order to persuade Latour to become a regular spy.

Latour finally agreed to become a spy and was driven to Moscow's Sheremetievo Airport, where he was put on an Aeroflot flight out of the country. Back in the West he courageously went straight to his employer and told him he had been subjected to a blackmail threat while in the Soviet Union. Away from the intimidating effect of the Lubyanka, he was able to see just how dangerous it would be to proceed any further along the path of treason. He was interrogated at length by French counterespionage officers of the Service de Documentation Extérieure et de Contre-Espionnage (SDECE). At first he tried to minimize the extent of his disclosures, but eventually the whole truth came out. The authorities were sympathetic, being perhaps more understanding of this form of human weakness than security officers from another country. They agreed to keep the story from his wife and to say only that he had been subjected to threats and intimidation, and solitary confinement in the Lubyanka. But for several years Latour was taken off all secret work and forbidden access to classified documents—prohibitions which greatly damaged his career prospects and professional work. In 1972, however, he was finally cleared of all suspicion and reinstated.

The sexpionage entrapment against Latour was a carefully planned operation, involving a large number of agents, a trained swallow, and highly sophisticated surveillance equipment. Not all KGB snares are so subtle. Sometimes the hidden camera is replaced by the crude expedient of having two KGB officers put their shoulders to a locked bedroom door and smash their way in. At this point photographs may or may not be taken. Sometimes the officers will play the roles of an outraged husband and his "best friend" who have come to expose the infidelity of a wife. On other occasions they will pretend to be ordinary police officers investigating an alleged rape.

This is what happened in the case of a thirty-one-year-old American engineer who visited Moscow during the summer of 1966. The KGB was well aware that the man was engaged in important top-secret research for the American Air Force. While dining at a restaurant in Kharkov he met an attractive Russian woman. They became acquainted over the meal and, afterwards, she suggested showing him some of the city sights. She led him down a winding path in a park to a secluded bench and they started to kiss. For a while she returned his eager embraces; then, suddenly, she started to scream. Flash guns exploded in the darkness close by and ten men sprang from surrounding bushes. One of them, who called himself Major Subolov, told the American that he would be charged with attempted rape unless he co-operated.

Like Latour he was flown to Moscow and locked up. After several days of isolation from Western officials and intensive interrogation, he agreed to co-operate. He then gave the KGB specialists details of his work. He also agreed to spy for the Russians, and was told to fly to Mexico City the following December to meet a KGB agent. Back in the United States, the American told the authorities what had happened. He lost his security clearance and his job as a result.

Such stories could be multiplied many times over and still form only the tip of the sexpionage iceberg. Western intelligence only learns of such entrapments when the victims either confess or are caught. Often an arrest comes only after years of successful looting of secret information for Moscow-based masters. It is very hard for counterintelligence to detect such treachery when there are no clear political or financial motives for the betrayal. Even when there are such indications, Western security can prove alarmingly lax. Junior officers living well above their salaries and senior government officials whose earlier allegiance to the Communist party is a matter of record have been able to operate in sensitive areas for years without coming under suspicion. In many cases the activities of a subverted national are discovered only because his country's intelligence service manages to subvert a Communist official, or because a highly placed Warsaw Pact intelligence officer defects of his own accord. It is only very occasionally that a victim has the courage to fight back, or a KGB sexpionage operation goes awry. This did happen in the early sixties, when the late President Sukarno of Indonesia triumphed magnificently over the system. It is a story which still raises smiles in Western intelligence circles.

With an international reputation as a ladies' man, the president seemed like an obvious target for a sex trap during a visit to Moscow. A number of beautiful women were introduced to him and they usually ended up in his bedroom where the hidden cameras filmed the proceedings. Towards the end of his visit the president was escorted to KGB headquarters where the films were played back to him as the prelude to blackmail. Dr. Sukarno beamed as the movies unrolled. When the show was over and the lights came up, he asked astounded KGB officials if it would be possible to have copies of the film made to take home with him for public showing. He is reported to have said: "My people are going to be so proud of me!"

But, according to CIA sources, a sexpionage plot against an Indonesian ambassador had a less happy ending. In 1963 the KGB snared their victim and a year later he paid the price for his liaison when he was forced to forward a series of forged documents to President Sukarno. The operation, devised by the Soviet Union but engineered through the Czech foreign intelligence service, the Statni Tajna Bezpecnost (STB), was a standard disinformation campaign aimed at turning Indonesian public opinion against the United States.

The documents which Sukarno accepted in good faith from his diplomat detailed various alleged CIA plots against his country, including a joint Anglo-American invasion from Malaysia. The president responded by making a series of strongly anti-Western speeches, and a mob attacked American property in Djakarta. But the campaign backfired on the Communists when their local members, misled like everybody else by the disinformation, attempted a coup. They expected that public opinion would be on their side when on September 30, 1965 they murdered six generals in a plan to take over the government. The anticipated popular uprising never materialized and the army exacted terrible revenge on the Communists. In the bloodbath that followed an estimated 50,000 were executed.

Although the Soviet Union has been making use of sexpionage with considerable success, especially in Germany, since 1945, it is only in the past ten years that the British and American governments have really awakened to the menace which such entrapments pose. Even today, their reaction when individuals pluck up the courage to admit they have been snared by a KGB sex trap, or when such a trap comes to light, plays straight into the hands of the Russians. Such men are often victimized by disgrace and dismissal, frequently for reasons which have more to do with outmoded concepts of morality than any security risk. This attitude is welcomed by the KGB, since it is far less likely that victims will confess voluntarily in the future, preferring to take the initially easy option of co-operating rather than face the immediate publicity and scandal.

The first indication that the British government was taking the threat of sexpionage seriously came in 1964. At this time the country's security services were reeling under the discovery of a Soviet espionage ring operating against the Naval Underwater Weapons Establishment at Portland, and the homosexual blackmail of Admiralty clerk William John Vassall. In response to these events Britain's counterintelligence organizations, then called MI-5 (today known as the Security Service), produced a pamphlet, *Their Trade Is Treachery*. It could have been of immense value to businessmen, scientists, and others whose work necessitated their traveling behind the Iron Curtain. However, largely for fear of upsetting the Russians, its circulation was confined to government departments. In ten chapters, with such headings as "How to Become a Spy in Six Easy Lessons" and "How Not to Become a Spy in Six Not-so-easy Lessons," the authors outlined many of the then-current KGB sexpionage techniques. Five years later the British Board of Trade produced a six-page booklet warning businessmen who intended to visit the Soviet Union about the risks of sexual blackmail. They dealt briefly with such techniques as infrared photography and telephone tapping. Similar cautions are issued to Americans with access to restricted information before they make a trip to any Communist country.

The Russian response to such publications is either to ignore them or to ridicule the dangers they pose. Satirizing the Board of Trade booklet, the famous Soviet satirical magazine *Krokodil* suggested that visiting businessmen worried about their sex appeal might try wearing woolen underpants to deter the ladies. "Can a man look really sexy in woolen pants?" inquired the *Krokodil* writer. Alternatively he suggested that visitors wear a kilt. "This will deprive you of female company. But it would be wise to start a moustache or beard to ward off Moscow males." As a final suggestion *Krokodil* told readers that foreigners could always travel around Moscow in a coffin loaded aboard a hearse. "The coffin would be carried into the place of business and the lid lifted off only long enough for the visitor to sign a lucrative contract!" Apart from these ploys, the best bet, the magazine concluded, was for businessmen to concentrate on their business and not get mixed up in anything shady. Commenting on the charge by one Western visitor that he had returned to his hotel and found a nude girl on the bed, *Krokodil* remarked, "He forgot to add that on the night in question he was so boozed up he could have seen not only a nude but a violet giraffe as well."

But for the KGB, sexpionage is a subject neither for humor nor ridicule. It is a serious and complex technique of subversion which occupies the time of thousands of staff officers, technicians, bed partners, and surveillance experts. They maintain special apartments in Moscow where entrapments can be carried out, have bedrooms fitted with photographic and electronic equipment in major hotels all over the Soviet Union, and run special sex schools where male and female bed partners are trained. Clearly the KGB has invested an enormous amount of money and time in the sexpionage industry. Has it paid off?

Later chapters will examine in detail major Soviet sexpionage operations against the West, but in general it can be said that the technique has allowed the KGB to carry out many major espionage coups which might otherwise have proved impossible. It has enabled their spies to steal a wide range of military and industrial secrets, to infiltrate NATO, and gain advanced warning of counterintelligence operations against their agents in Europe.

While Western governments seem to have been slow to realize and respond to the dangers of sexpionage, they have been equally reluctant to use these methods themselves and it is interesting to consider why this has been. The simplest, and certainly the most agreeable, answer would be that Western security services are more moral—that they consider such tactics beneath them. In the wake of Watergate and in the light of disclosures about British secret-service operations in Northern Ireland, this view seems less naive than disingenuous. Why then has the West only dipped its toes in these murky waters while the Soviet Union has been wallowing there for decades?

There are two main reasons, both stemming from the very different societies in which the services operate.

The Russians are, I believe, psychologically attracted to sexpionage because of the antipermissive nature of their present culture. Many of their leaders were brought up to regard overt sexuality as wicked, and regard any form of license, along with pornography, to be the fruit of degenerate capitalism. This leads to the conscious conclusion that sexpionage will be an especially effective weapon against Westerners, and the unconscious projection of the repressed sexuality onto their enemies. In addition, sexpionage enables them to indulge in vicarious sexual adventures, to arrange liaisons, and look at pictures of intercourse in the course of duty. They are thus able to enjoy pornography at second hand without guilt, in much the same way that an advocate of censorship will study blue films.

Western intelligence agencies, appraising the technique more objectively, see it as a potentially effective but alarmingly double-edged weapon. They know all too well the press interest and political furor likely to arise if a major sexpionage operation were discovered. So operations executives are circumspect. They use defensive sexpionage, supplying women to VIPs and others under circumstances where the need to *protect* a visiting statesman or ambassador from the risk of blackmail arises regularly. They use offensive sexpionage, as a means of obtaining a blackmail hold, sparingly and only under circumstances where the maximum amount of security can be guaranteed. This usually means in areas where military or police control is well established and where the media and similar organs of public investigation and opinion can be silenced—for example, as I shall explain in Chapter Nine, the British use of offensive sexpionage in Belfast.

There is some evidence that the CIA made use of offensive sexpionage, on a limited scale, during the Nixon era. In February 1975, for example, Washington columnist Jack Anderson reported that the Central Intelligence Agency had set up a series of "love nests" in luxury apartments around the United States. One such trap was said to have been established in a Greenwich Village high-rise building, where a camera was hidden behind a picture of sailing ships. Foreign diplomats romping with agency-supplied call girls were said to have been filmed and blackmailed. Another disclosure in the press linked a voluptuous Cuban girl, Marie Lorenz, with a sexpionage plot to steal secrets from Fidel Castro. She was said to have acted a Mata Hari role, sleeping with the Cuban leader and stealing secrets for the agency when the opportunity arose.

Whatever truth there was in these stories, and it is possible that the CIA-supplied apartments were, in fact, part of a defensive sexpionage operation, the use of this technique as a major instrument of spying and subversion does not exist, I believe, outside the Soviet bloc. It is for this reason, rather than any anti-Soviet bias, that the bulk of this book deals with the extensive and elaborate sexpionage traps mounted by the KGB with the co-operation of other Communist secret service organizations. These services operate within closed societies where the media publishes what the government directs and where no journalist could ask awkward questions and survive—societies in which the cult of security is an all-powerful and all-pervading fact of life.

2

The Spider of Dzerzhinsky Square

A tall gray stone building at 2 Dzerzhinsky Square, Moscow is the headquarters of the world's most powerful secret service organization, the Komitet Gosudarstvennoy Bezopasnosti, or KGB.

The KGB, a state within a state, was described by Allen Dulles as "a multi-purpose clandestine arm of power more than an intelligence and counterintelligence organization. It is an instrument for subversion, manipulation, and violence, for the secret intervention in the affairs of other countries."

This awe-inspiring organization which employs some 90,000 staff officers in addition to hundreds of thousands of part-time agents is a logical development of the concept of a scientific dictatorship, which Lenin defined in 1920 as "no more nor less than unlimited power resting directly on force, not limited by anything nor restrained by any laws or absolute rules."

The KGB's penetration of Soviet society is absolute. The web spun from Dzerzhinsky Square spreads across every region of the USSR and ensnares each of its 250 million citizens. In his study of the KGB, American writer John Barron surmised what would happen if it were suddenly to vanish. With its passing, he says, the Politburo would lose "the basic means of regulating Soviet thought, speech, and behavior, of controlling the arts, science, religion, education, the press, police, and military. Gone too would be the most effective means of suppressing ethnic minorities, of preventing the flight of Soviet citizens, of keeping watch on individuals, or compelling the whole populace to subserve the interests of the Soviet rulers. . . . The Soviet Union would lose most of its capacity to commit espionage abroad, to subvert public officials, to plot sabotage and assassination, to foment strikes, demonstrations, and riots. To nurture terrorism and guerrilla warfare; to clandestinely pollute public discourse with misinformation and calumny."

The foundations of the modern KGB were laid long before the 1917 Revolution, by Czar Ivan the Terrible in the sixteenth century. During the next three hundred years the Russian secret police evolved as an instrument by which successive czars suppressed home-grown revolutionaries and countered foreign espionage.

In 1881, following the assassination of Czar Alexander II, the Okhrana or Department of State Protection, was set up on the lines of the efficient German secret service. Its agents were soon active abroad. In 1883 Okhrana spies went to America for the first time to keep watch on Vladimir Legaev, a former member of the Okhrana.

The Okhrana encouraged informers at all levels of society. "Its aim was to turn Russia into a nation of spies," says Richard Deacon in his study of the Russian secret service. "Thus espionage became an essay in mass observation. The result was that by the end of the century tens of thousands of people all over Russia, possibly even more than a hundred thousand, had at some time or other either been members of the Okhrana or informers. It was rare to find a single family that did not possess an informer among its members."

It is important to bear in mind this tradition of betrayal and the climate of fear and suspicion which it produces when considering the present-day activities of the KGB.

As well as creating a network of informers, the Okhrana was methodically building up a card index system on its enemies. Every item of personal and identifying detail was included in the files. A neatly written entry on the card of a revolutionary named Joseph Dzhugashvili, for instance, noted that he had a slightly webbed left foot, "the second and third toes having grown together." Dzhugashvili later changed his name to Joseph Stalin.

These days such information is contained in constantly up-dated dossiers stored on magnetic tape in the vast computer archives, located within steel and concrete vaults deep under Dzerzhinsky Square. At the touch of a button a technician in the reference section of the Center can set the tape spools spinning and the teleprinters clattering out the personal details on any one of an estimated 10 million men and women.

On December 20, 1917, the Bolsheviks renamed the Okhrana the

THE SPIDER OF DZERZHINSKY SQUARE

Cheka (Chrezvychainaya Komissiya po Borbe s Kontrrevolutsiei i Sabotazham or Extraordinary Commission for Combating Counterrevolution and Sabotage).*

The Cheka's first chief was Feliks Edmundovich Dzerzhinsky, the founding father of modern-day Soviet espionage and subversion. Dzerzhinsky was born in 1877 to a Polish family who owned large estates near Vilna. As a youth he was religious and thought of becoming a priest. But while a student, his interest switched to politics. First he joined the Socialist Revolutionary party and then, growing impatient with their approach and objectives, he switched to the Bolsheviks.

Dzerzhinsky rose quickly in the party. Although a ruthless and gifted administrator, he was not an individual who could work under supervision or as a member of a team. When Lenin asked him to head the Cheka, he agreed only on the condition he be given total power over the secret service. Such was Lenin's regard for Dzerzhinsky's abilities that he agreed without hesitation. Under Dzerzhinsky the Cheka became a ruthlessly efficient instrument of the party, which tortured, imprisoned, and executed without mercy. The Cheka lived on betrayal and confession; the brutal punishments which were the inevitable end products of their operations were of only casual interest to the Chekists. As long as the monthly quota of "Enemies of the State" was arrested, the fate of the victims hardly bothered them.

Dzerzhinsky died of a heart attack in 1926, and the square outside his headquarters was renamed in his honor. Many of the secret service chiefs who followed him were less fortunate, both in the honors afforded them and in the peaceful manner of their end. Vyacheslav Menzhinsky, who took over after Dzerzhinsky's death, was probably poisoned by his ambitious successor, Henrik Yagoda. In 1936, Yagoda was removed from office after a dispute with Stalin, who was taking an increasing personal interest in the service. In 1938 Yagoda was shot.

Yagoda was succeeded by Nikolai Yezhov, an ambitious bureaucrat who vastly expanded the KGB under Stalin's direction. This was no

---

*In the decades that followed, the service was successively known as the GPU, the OGPU, the KNVO, the NKSS, the MGB, and the MOOP before being named the KGB (Komitet Gosudarstvennoy Bezopasnosti) in 1954. Even today, despite the endless succession of changes, KGB officers are known as Chekists by Soviet citizens. In this book, for the sake of simplicity, the Russian secret service will be referred to simply as the KGB

easy task, for while he recruited more staff in one operation, he was busy arresting and liquidating hundreds of old revolutionary officers in another. In some large departments only a fortunate few survived as the scythe of Stalin's paranoiac suspicions swept through the service. The machine, growing tired of cropping the terrified populace, was eating its own attendants. Yezhov was a merciless man, instantly and absolutely obedient to the demands of Stalin. But eventually the double-dealing and the bloody purges, which inspired within the ranks of the KGB a nervous hysteria from which it has still not completely recovered, proved too much even for him. Many of Yezhov's closest associates were convinced, towards the end, that he had gone completely mad. General Walter Krivitsky, a KGB agent who defected to the West in the late thirties, remembers that "in the middle of an important and confidential telephone call, Yezhov would suddenly burst out in crazy laughter and tell stories of his own life in the most obscene language." In 1938 Yezhov was removed to a lunatic asylum and later executed.

He was replaced by a cold, sinister, and supremely efficient chief, Lavrenti Pavlovich Beria. Like Stalin, Beria was a Georgian, born in Tiflis in 1898. The son of a civil servant, Beria overcame the handicap of poor eyesight to serve in the Czar's army. After the Revolution he became a Soviet secret agent working in Prague and Paris. He ingeniously penetrated Russian émigré circles, gaining confidences and secrets while posing as a Socialist intellectual of moderate views. "It was this quality for patiently infiltrating the enemy's ranks which made him so indispensable to Stalin," says Richard Deacon. "While others lacked the nerve and talents to anticipate Stalin's every whim, Beria unfailingly knew what his master wanted and which way the Central Committee was likely to go next."

While Stalin survived, Beria was safe. The purges of 1934 and 1936 left him unharmed and, indeed, strengthened his position inside the secret service. By March 1938, and the "Trial of the Twenty-one," after which eighteen high-ranking officers were executed, some 500 members of the secret service had been shot. Beria was given the enormous job of rebuilding a shattered, demoralized organization. Other men might have been appalled by the magnitude of the task, but Beria had no hesitation. He was convinced that war was imminent and concentrated the efforts of his service on obtaining military intelligence. He also rapidly expanded the index system, ordering overseas agents to provide data for dossiers on an increasingly wide range of people. No longer was the service interested only in possible revolutionaries. Now files were opened on journalists, university lecturers, diplomats, politicians, economists, scientists, and a hundred other professional people in every major country in the world. It was Lavrenti Beria who first began to develop sexpionage as a powerful weapon of subversion. His interest in the technique may, in part, have sprung from his perverted sexual make-up; he liked his girls very young.

In January 1946, there were a number of internal changes. The MGB or Ministry of State Security (Ministerstvo Gosudarstvennoy Bezopasnosti) was created, and the NKVD became the Ministry of Internal Affairs. Beria remained in effective control of both organizations until Stalin's death on March 5, 1953.

The present chief of the KGB, Yuri Vladimirovich Andropov, was appointed to the post in May 1967. A close friend of Leonid Brezhnev, Andropov has an apartment on Kutuzovsky Prospekt in the same building as Leonid Brezhnev. An accomplished diplomat and convincing talker, Andropov was the Soviet ambassador to Hungary during the abortive uprising. After personally guaranteeing the safety of a Hungarian delegation led by General Pál Maleter, Andropov persuaded the group to attend talks with three Soviet generals. The discussion went remarkably well and agreement was reached over a wide range of issues. By way of celebration the Soviet generals invited Maléter and his party to a banquet. As they sat eating, General Ivan Serov, accompanied by a small army of KGB men, broke into the room and informed the Hungarians that they were under arrest. They were later executed.

A tall, slightly reserved man, Andropov was born at the start of World War I in northwest Russia, close to the Finnish border, and was educated at the State University of Petrozavodsk, the industrial capital city of the Karelo-Finnish Republic.

In his teens he worked as a cinema projectionist and for the post office, but his interest in the Communist party soon led to his taking on a full-time job organizing the Komsomol, the Communist Youth League. By 1939 he was Komsomol chief in the city of Yaroslavl. During the war he became a guerrilla fighter, organizing partisan units behind the German lines. After the war he continued his political career. In 1951 he was head of a political department of the Central Committee in Moscow, and two years later went to Budapest as an "adviser"; a year later he was appointed ambassador. A careful and ambitious man, well aware of the dangers involved in aiming at political power in the Soviet Union,

Andropov has the useful knack of backing the right horses. During a party power struggle he supported Leonid Brezhnev; later his reward was the appointment by Brezhnev as head of the KGB.

Shortly after 8:30 A.M. each weekday a KGB limousine arrives outside his apartment and drives him to Dzerzhinsky Square, where he takes the elevator to a large office on the third floor. Compared with those of his subordinates, Andropov's suite is lavishly appointed. Oriental rugs cover the thick carpet and the walls are paneled in mahogany. A door, near his large desk, leads to a private bedroom and bathroom. Behind the desk hangs a massive oil portrait of Feliks Dzerzhinsky in a heavy gilt frame. On the desk stands a battery of colored phones; one is connected directly to the office of Leonid Brezhnev.

What is life like inside this rococo building a couple of blocks from the Kremlin?

The morning shift takes over from the night staff at nine o'clock, but an hour beforehand employees are starting to stream across the square from the two subway stations close by to take advantage of the cheap breakfasts to which they are entitled.

Many of the staff members occupy cramped, rather shabby offices in the old nineteenth-century block which is built around a courtyard. Overlooking one side of this enclosed yard are the tiny barred windows of the Lubyanka prison, which has housed such notable KGB prisoners as the American spy-plane pilot Gary Powers and the British agent Greville Wynne. Ironically, the cells have also held many high-ranking KGB men who fell from power and favor during one of the regular purges of the Stalin era. Most of them only made two short journeys after their arrest. The first was from their offices to the cellblock, the second from their cells to the execution chamber of the Lubyanka.

The building started life as the offices of the All-Russian Insurance Company; later it was converted into a hotel for a short time before becoming secret-service headquarters in 1918. During the inter-war years, the service expanded beyond the capacity of the old building and in 1945, to ease the acute accommodation problem and provide room for a further increase in staff, office blocks adjoining Number 2 Dzerzhinsky Square were demolished and a modern nine-story extension was constructed by Soviet political prisoners and German POWs. A further indication of the expansionist ambitions of the KGB is the departure in 1972 of the First Chief Directorate for its sparkling new offices just outside the city center which house an estimated 10,000 officers and support staff. In addition to the main blocks, the KGB also controls other buildings around the square. At Number 12 is the officers' club, where senior KGB men hold private parties to celebrate some particularly impressive espionage coup. A few of the smaller specialist departments are located away from Dzerzhinsky Square. For example, the section controlling the swallows and their male counterparts, the "ravens," has a five-story block disguised as a warehouse in central Moscow.

Internally, KGB headquarters are little different from government offices anywhere in the world. The walls are painted an institutional light green; the floors are bare parquet except in the offices of senior men who are entitled to regulation carpeting. The furnishings are heavy and well worn. A typical office will have some upright chairs, perhaps a slightly shabby leather armchair, and a wooden desk dominated by an array of telephones. The most conspicuous item in any KGB office is a large safe with a combination lock. Standing orders demand that all classified documents must be locked away at night and the safe then sealed with wax as a further security precaution. Under Andropov's command is a complicated bureaucratic structure—rigidly compartmentalized, immensely powerful, and endowed by the Soviet leadership with vast resources and enormous responsibilities. Above him Andropov has only the Central Committee of the Communist party and the Politburo. Actual control is by the latter, that of the Council of Ministers being purely nominal. The *political* control is so strong and pervasive that it seems unlikely the KGB could ever break its leash and turn against its masters. These controls also ensure that all operations faithfully reflect the calculated desires of the ruling oligarchy. Thus, no matter how brutal or dangerous, the actions of the KGB should not be regarded as unauthorized.

The service is organized into four Chief Directorates, the First, Second, Fifth, and a Border Guards Directorate; seven independent Directorates and six independent Departments. These are further subdivided into sections called variously, Departments, Directorates, Services and Directions.

As far as sexpionage operations are concerned, the activities of the First and Second Chief Directorates are most important.

The First Chief Directorate has the task of organizing all Soviet operations abroad; these include espionage, disinformation, assassination, and subversion, but exclude military intelligence, which is undertaken by the GRU.* For convenience the world is divided into ten geographic areas, each of which is looked after by a different department within the First Chief Directorate. The first department has responsibility for the United States and Canada; the second for Latin America; the third for the United Kingdom, Commonwealth countries, and Scandinavia; the fourth and fifth for Germany, Austria, France, Spain, Italy, Belgium, Holland, Luxembourg, and Ireland. In addition, the First Chief Directorate contains numerous special subdivisions. Directorate T has the task of assessing technical intelligence and directing espionage operations against such targets as nuclear research stations and electronics laboratories. It employs many top Soviet scientists, and the great increase in industrial espionage during the sixties can be traced back to the formation of this directorate in 1963.

Another key subdivision is Directorate S or the "illegals" directorate. Illegals are spies working abroad under cover and without diplomatic immunity. If they get caught they are usually jailed, although they may be quietly swapped for a captured Western agent. Colonel Rudolf Ivanovich Abel was a top KGB illegal, as were Morris and Lona Cohen, known as the Krogers, who spied on Britain.

The most sinister of all departments within the First Chief Directorate is undoubtedly Department V, also known as the executive action department, which arranges assassinations and organizes acts of sabotage.†

Apart from these operational departments, the First Chief Directorate has sections concerned with codes and ciphers; communications, including communication satellites; and the maintenance of contact with agents abroad. Frequently this is done through commercial broadcasts on Radio Moscow. The coded messages are sent on designated nights

---

*The GRU (Glavnoye Razvedyvatelnoye Upravleniye) is the Chief Intelligence Directorate of the Soviet Military Staff—the fourth department of the General Staff of the Red Army. It was built up by Leon Trotsky, with the aid of Captain George Hill of British Military Intelligence, when he discovered that Felix Dzerzhinsky kept a dossier on him. There is intense rivalry between the KGB and the GRU. Both have agents operating under diplomatic cover. Oleg Penkovsky was a GRU colonel arrested in October 1962 and shot for spying for the SIS and CIA.

†East and West have developed their own euphemisms for such activities. The CIA refers to an action in which blood is shed as "wet work." The KGB terms the activities of Department V *mokrie dela*, literally "wet affairs." The SIS phrase most frequently used is 'termination with extreme prejudice "

and agents are alerted by the playing of a special tune. Frank Bossard, a KGB spy in Britain's Ministry of Defense, had to listen for the "Saber Dance," and German sex spy Heinz Suetterlin was given his orders after "Moscow Nights" had been played.

The task of the Second Chief Directorate is to supervise and subvert foreign visitors and to control the lives of Soviet citizens at home. There are twelve departments, the first six being concerned with Soviet-based foreign diplomats, an indication of the importance the KGB gives to this form of espionage. The first department has responsibility for diplomats from the United States and Latin America; the second those from the UK and the British Commonwealth.

In addition to these departments the Second Chief Directorate has a large technical-support group, which employs photographers and bugging experts, locksmiths, safe-crackers and pickpockets. An Industrial Security Directorate monitors work being done in Western laboratories and technical institutes, and compiles lists of scientists and other technicians who will be worth watching and, whenever possible, placing in blackmail situations.

The Second Chief Directorate is also responsible for the recruitment and training of swallow and raven sex spies. Comfortable apartments fitted with permanent electronic and photographic equipment are maintained by the directorate in Moscow and other major Soviet cities where these agents set up temporary home during sexpionage operations. When a fast entrapment has to be organized it is usual for hotel rooms, which are also permanently set up for recording and photography, to be used. If it proves impossible to manipulate a visitor into one of these special rooms, then another may be temporarily bugged. A locksmith from the Technical Support Division will break into the room, in those cases where the hotel management is not to be informed of the operation, and a bugging technician goes to work. Planting a radio microphone takes less than five minutes. A usual technique is to fit a special transmitter inside the bedside telephone which then relays any sound in the room to a nearby receiver. Hiding a camera is more difficult and requires much greater preparation.

Five years ago a camera loaded with film was needed; today a miniature TV camera may be used instead. Although the image quality is inferior to film systems, the ease and speed of installation combined with the low light levels in which the equipment can function are telling advantages. Furthermore the entire entrapment can be recorded on video tape, making it certain that incriminating evidence will be obtained. When still cameras are used, it has happened that all thirty-six frames on a 35mm film strip showed nothing more interesting than the victim taking off his shoes and tie.

If there is no time for such planting, the KGB will arrange the entrapment so that something incriminating happens either out of doors or at a time when agents can elbow their way into the room.

Typical scenarios for these operations are as follows. An unsuspecting visitor meets an attractive woman and spends the evening with her. As they are walking back to his hotel she will choose a suitably deserted street and start to kiss him. When he responds she will struggle, tear her dress, and scream "rape." Instantly half a dozen "police officers" will surround the horrified man and threaten to charge him with a serious assault. In the second instance the swallow, or raven, will alert the KGB at the right moment by calling out a prearranged code word. The lock will then be smashed and the officials, one armed with a camera and flash gun, will burst in. During such operations the KGB agents may pose as ordinary police officers or outraged husbands after divorce evidence.

For Tania, as for the other KGB operatives involved in such entrapments, their participation is just part of their work. Almost certainly Tania felt no affection for her target, and her passion in bed was as contrived as their meeting. Like most experienced prostitutes Tania was able to perform convincingly while remaining emotionally detached. Yet her task was, in some ways, far harder than that of an ordinary call girl, for she had to make love not merely to please Latour but to satisfy the unseen KGB cameraman. She had to ensure that Latour's face was turned towards the photographer so that the blackmail would be effective. She had to perform in a completely uninhibited manner while knowing that every intimate detail was being recorded. That she could do so was a tribute to the bizarre and humiliating training she had received at one of the KGB's schools for love.

3

Secrets of the Sex Schools

Now in her mid-fifties, Lydia Kuzazova is still a remarkably attractive woman. Tall, blonde, and elegant, she has clear blue eyes and a charm which most men find irresistible. With her cool sophistication she might be the wife of a senior diplomat or a successful business executive. In fact, Lydia is an unmarried colonel in the KGB and headmistress of an astonishing school for sex spies situated in a desolate area of Russia at Verkhonoye, near the city of Kazan.

In this barrack-like complex, swallows and ravens from all over Russia are groomed in the techniques of sexpionage. It is a degrading training course designed to strip them of every sexual inhibition. They are taught how to give their partners maximum pleasure, how to perform and apparently enjoy every possible variation and perversion of the sex act, and how to behave naturally even though they are aware their every move is being filmed by hidden cameras.

Lydia Kuzazova herself knows only too well how to practice what she now teaches. A former swallow, she was sent into West Germany in the early 1950s to set up a sexpionage ring in Frankfurt. With ample funds provided by the KGB, she established a luxurious massage and beauty parlor near the city center. It was extravagantly decorated and extremely discreet. Lydia recruited the most beautiful girls in the area and paid them well to perform as high-class prostitutes and not ask too many questions. Soon her "parlor" was attracting important industrialists, service diplomats, high-ranking army officers, and government officials. Regular clients were escorted through the respectable front rooms, where nothing in the least bit salacious ever took place, to comfortably appointed private cubicles in the back of the building. There her girls would first undress the client and then themselves before providing any type of "massage" which the customer demanded, from oral sex to normal intercourse. Considering the beauty of her girls and the lavishness of the surroundings, Lydia's prices were extremely modest: high enough to keep the establishment exclusive, yet reasonable enough for the well-off to patronize her regularly. What none of these clients realized was that concealed microphones and hidden cameras recorded their most intimate moments. Any indiscretion they uttered was taken down on tape recorders housed in a small back room to which Lydia had the only key. Rolls of 16mm film taken on the concealed movie cameras were smuggled back to East Germany for processing. They were then either used immediately to blackmail victims into revealing secrets, or held for future reference, to be used as blackmail material when the subject was promoted to a position which gave him access to valuable information. Although she provided the KGB with a wide range of general intelligence through blackmail and the indiscretion of her clients, Lydia's posting to Frankfurt had been with a very specific target in mind. Her orders were to subvert a suitably placed employee of the CIA's main European training and operations center, Camp David, which stood on a twelve-acre site at Oberurzel, ten miles from the city.

Outwardly Camp David looked like any other US Army establishment; but within its heavily guarded compound European and American agents were trained for operations behind the Iron Curtain. From its central control blocks spread an intricate network of agents, couriers, and informers which stretched deep into the heart of the Soviet Union. Lydia's assignment was to penetrate Camp David and discover its secrets. She succeeded magnificently.

The camp produced two types of agent, known as "blacks" and "grays." Blacks were full-time spies: men and women who operated in the Soviet bloc under false identities, with completely bogus reasons for going to their target Communist country. The grays were part-time agents: businessmen, journalists, and tourists who agreed to carry out single espionage missions in return for cash. But whether gray or black, all Camp David agents were carefully debriefed on their return from a mission and a routine part of this debriefing was taking a lie-detector test. One of these machines was operated by a forty-four-year-old US sergeant, Glen Rohrer, who had been posted to Camp David in 1955. Because of his job he had been present at hundreds of debriefing sessions. He knew the names and cover identities of virtually every CIA agent who had passed through the camp. He knew their methods of operating, their contacts, and their successes.

Early in 1960 Glen Rohrer visited Lydia's parlor. Like all agent handlers, he had been screened by the CIA before being sent to Camp David. Rohrer, according to the stringent security regulations at the camp, would have been dismissed from his highly sensitive job had he married a foreign national. As a single man he was allowed to date the same woman only three times. After living nearly six years under these abnormal conditions, Sergeant Rohrer was a lonely and frustrated man. Lydia's parlor seemed like the answer to his dreams, but he was careful to keep his liaisons with her attractive and understanding girls a secret from his superiors at the camp.

Rohrer was filmed and then blackmailed into providing Lydia with information about an agent who had just returned from East Germany. At first he co-operated reluctantly, then with less reserve. By 1965 he was willingly supplying the KGB with names and addresses. In August 1965, Lydia was alerted by a KGB agent in West German counterintelligence that the CIA was closing in on Rohrer. She tipped him off in time and Rohrer fled to Czechoslovakia. His abandoned car was found not far from the frontier and bloodhounds followed his scent right up to the barbed-wire border fence.

Rohrer's treachery was a staggering setback to Western intelligence. The work of twenty years was smashed and hundreds of agents were arrested. Lydia, her own safety at risk, was ordered to report back to Moscow. The parlor closed its doors for the last time and she returned in triumph to receive a promotion to colonel. For a few years she worked in Dzerzhinsky Square, advising on sexpionage entrapments in West Germany; then she was offered the important post of director of the Verkhonoye sex-spy school. She now divides her time between that house of love and a smaller spy school in Leningrad which operates from a palatial old building on the Nachimov Prospekt.

The girls trained by Lydia come from all over the Soviet Union. Before they are even approached by KGB recruiters, their backgrounds are meticulously investigated to make sure they are politically reliable. Beauty is obviously a primary qualification, but they must also have brains and charm. The ability to be accepted at all levels of society is essential, and knowledge of a foreign language, preferably English, French or German, increases a girl's chances of acceptance. Since training in foreign languages forms an important part of every child's education in the Soviet Union, this last qualification is invariably satisfied.

After a girl has been selected for possible training as a swallow, she is called to a private meeting by a KGB recruiter. At first no mention is made of sex. She is told only that her name has been put forward for a well-paid job in the party machine. If she accepts, the recruiter tells her, the material rewards will be considerable. In addition to a good salary there will be a flat in Moscow or one of the other major cities, and other attractive fringe benefits. She is then given some time to think things over while the KGB makes further checks on her family. During a subsequent meeting she is given a few more details and warned that the job involves access to important state secrets. Once she agrees to take the training she is cautioned she must never reveal what she knows, not even to her closest relatives. She is then sent for the four-month-long preliminary selection course at the Marx-Engels School outside Moscow. If this proves satisfactory the girl is transferred to one of the sex schools for further training.

Ravens are selected on much the same basis as swallows. Not all of them are strikingly handsome men, as the KGB is well aware that bored middle-aged women, the likely targets for ravens, are not necessarily attracted by physical good looks. The men are selected by women KGB officers on the basis of their personality and sex appeal. Some are relatively young men, others middle-aged with established careers in the arts, journalism, or industry. Where ravens are concerned the KGB is far more likely to make use of part-timers for heterosexual entrapments. Homosexuals are also trained to play their part in sexpionage with targets who are homosexual members of foreign embassies and tourists. These are almost exclusively full-time agents, often male prostitutes who are given a choice between working for the KGB or being imprisoned.

Training in the techniques of sexual entrapment also forms an important part of the ten-year-long course which top KGB illegals undergo before being sent abroad to establish spy rings. Groomed to fit into their new environment socially and sexually, they receive lectures on the sexual mores and attitudes of the country in which they will be living. They read men's magazines from that country and study the way its newspapers deal with sex stories. They watch many of the films currently being shown there, normal commercial films, underground movies, and a se-

SECRETS OF THE SEX SCHOOLS

lection of pornographic films in order to see the kind of sexual behavior most characteristic of that country.

Their studying is done in an environment elaborately contrived to correspond as closely as possible to that of their assigned country. This has involved the KGB in the construction of astonishing fake towns where every detail of the life-style of various foreign countries has been duplicated, including such items as currency, bus tickets, and food prices.

Prior to his defection to the West in the mid-sixties, Anatoli Sorokin had worked for Department S of the KGB's First Chief Directorate. He told me the environment is more like a film set than a real town. Every detail is correct just as it would be in a well-made film. There is a main street with brick buildings on either side. The street is about 200 yards long. There are shops, a cinema, a supermarket, and a bank. During training sessions the area is filled with people dressed to represent typical characters from the country under study. For example, on the British set there would be policemen, a postman, a butcher serving in his shop. There is a bus with a conductor so that agents can practice asking for the correct fares and stating their destinations knowledgeably. There is a post office where they can go to buy stamps, postal orders, and so on. Another set represents an English village with a pub and general store. The whole area is surrounded by barbed-wire fences and patrolled by armed guards with dogs.

Details of this amazing top secret KGB reconstruction of a slice of urban and rural England, which forms part of the Gaczyna finishing school for spies, first came to the West in a report prepared by a Scandinavian intelligence man, Major Per Lindgren. An officer with the Swedish General Staff, Lindgren somehow managed to penetrate the tight security and enjoy a conducted tour of the entire training center. Dubbed "Clifton" or "Seaville" by Western intelligence agencies, this school has turned out such ace KGB illegals as Colonel Abel and Konon Trofimovich Molody, who operated in England under the cover name of Gordon Lonsdale.

Since Lindgren's report, further information about Gaczyna has become available from Soviet defectors, including the defector I interviewed in Bayswater, London. Although it is impossible to place total reliance on such information, there is no doubt that Gaczyna and another similar spy school, the Prakhovka near Minsk, contain amazingly realistic reconstructions of European and American environments.

Gaczyna is said to be situated about one hundred miles southwest of

Kuibyshev, a city of 800,000 inhabitants, and to cover an area of about 400 square miles in a remote region near the border of two of the Soviet Union's fifteen autonomous republics. The local people believe it to be a military research center. Inside the perimeter fence, which is guarded by armed KGB men, a lonely road runs through a thirty-mile no man's land. At the end of this desolate *cordon sanitaire* there is a second fence and another checkpoint.

Gaczyna is divided into four sections, each sealed off from the others by high fences, patroling guards, and a wide neutral zone. Each section is equipped with its own instructors and fake towns and villages. In the two northern sectors spies are trained for operations against North America and Canada in one area, and the United Kingdom in the adjoining section. The southern sections cover Australia, New Zealand, and South Africa. Agents assigned to operate against Germany, Austria, Scandinavia, and Switzerland receive similar final training at the Prakhovka spy school, which covers some 200 square miles and is located seventy miles north east of Minsk.

Attention to detail is meticulous. Only the language of the country under study may be spoken and many of the people who populate these reconstructions were born in the country whose way of life they now endeavor to act out. All the goods sold in shops are imported directly from the country concerned, as are books, magazines, newspapers, bus tickets, stamps, postal orders, and advertising posters. The cinemas show a wide range of films and a closed-circuit television network pipes in appropriate programs. In the British sector the KGB spies were the first Soviet citizens to enjoy such epics as "The Forsythe Saga"—although they had to watch it without the benefit of subtitles. "Coronation Street" is used by the instructors as an illustration of working-class life. These and other programs are video-taped in the Soviet Embassy in Kensington and the tapes are then shipped out by the KGB Resident in the diplomatic pouch. Radio programs are also tape-recorded for use at the schools. "The Archers" (a soap-opera radio program about a farming community) is followed avidly by the inhabitants of the English section of Gaczyna. A note supplied with the program warns that it promotes British Ministry of Agriculture propaganda not necessarily reflecting the opinions of British farmers!

The merchandise in each area is continuously updated in the light of information supplied by KGB men in the actual country concerned. Recent inflation in the West, for example, has meant a great deal of extra work for KGB agents abroad. Each week they travel around the shops in major and provincial cities checking increases in prices and forwarding the information to Dzerzhinsky Square so that the price tags in the training areas can be adjusted accordingly.

During training sessions KGB agents are given a typical weekly wage on which they have to live. They practice renting small apartments and rooms, and even live in them for days at a stretch. They practice ordering restaurant meals, buying cinema tickets, and hiring cabs. Their instructors throw parties at which the alcohol flows freely. But even when drunk the agent must keep up his act. If he makes a mistake or, worst of all, slips back into his mother tongue, the punishments are severe. They range from heavy fines to dismissal from the course.

But before any of these agents reach the final training areas, they will have gone through a stringent process of selection and elimination so that only the very best make it to the top. According to writer Bernard Hutton, a former member of the Central Committee of the Czech Communist party and now a leading anti-Communist author, the instruction begins with a four-month-long selection and political indoctrination course at the Marx-Engels School at Gorky, near Moscow. Most of the young men and women who pass through the heavily guarded doors of the Marx-Engels School have no idea that they are being groomed for a career in espionage. They believe that the detailed KGB checks on their backgrounds, political views, and private lives which preceded their acceptance to the course were merely signs that they were being considered for important party positions.

The Marx-Engels School stands well back from the main road and is screened by a high wall. During the course discipline is strict and, on arrival, all personal identity papers and party membership cards must be surrendered. The intention is to make the students stop thinking and behaving as individuals and to start identifying only with the teams to which they are assigned. The working day starts with breakfast at seven o'clock and ends with a final lecture at ten o'clock at night. There are two breaks for meals and two fifteen-minute rest periods for light refreshment. Apart from these moments of relaxation it is all hard work, with instructors constantly on the alert for signs of physical or ideological weakness. The young men and women, whose average age is eighteen, sleep in mixed dormitories and share communal showers. But there is very little time to think about sex and at night they are usually too exhausted to do anything except sleep

From the dozens who arrive to start each course, only a few are selected for the second part of the training, which takes place in the Lenin Technical High School. These courses are held in a complex of buildings and training areas covering some seven square miles, approached by a long, narrow road which runs through bleak countryside. This school is located at Verkhonoye, about 100 miles from Kazan near the Tatar Autonomous Soviet Republic. Like the other training areas, it is guarded by fences, dogs, and armed troops. Life at the Lenin Technical School is every bit as spartan and strict as at the Marx-Engels School. Students live in long, somber blocks; personal possessions are kept to a minimum, and the iron-frame beds in the long dormitories are only separated by narrow metal lockers. The emphasis at the Lenin Technical School is on physical and mental fitness. The students are turned out at dawn to go on long, muscle-tearing cross-country runs through the rocky training area. They take special physical-education courses which range from parachuting to driving a car at high speeds. Unarmed combat is an important part of the program and a training manual prepared by the KGB for use in the school states bluntly, "Any form of violence must be introduced when other methods of persuasion fail, if necessary, in the interest of the cause."

In 1970 an important defector named Sasha Demidov reached the West and provided intelligence officers with a detailed inside look at life in the Lenin Technical School. The son of a Czech army officer, Demidov was selected for training by the KGB because he spoke fluent Russian and because his mother had been born in Moscow. He was sent to the spy school in 1966, and recalls that the "uniform" consisted of slacks, sweaters, and gym shoes. "No one wore badges of rank, but we were subjected to the strictest discipline. Instruction was usually given to a class of about thirty, but there were smaller groups for special courses. Now and then an instructor was sent out from Moscow for special top-secret training. The basic course included politics, economics, criminology, codes and ciphers, photography, and methods for making and cultivating contacts."

The sinister nature of their future profession was constantly being emphasized. "Lessons were divided into two categories," said Demidov, "what they called *chistaya rabota*, clean work, and *gryaznaya rabota*, dirty work. Clean work included recruiting methods to be used with people who were willing to work for the Soviet Union out of ideological motives. Dirty work included the techniques of bribery, extortion, and blackmail. We were shown how to set up sexpionage entrapments and how to obtain evidence." After lectures in dirty work, the students would have to put theory into practice. Although they would be using mainly professional swallows and ravens to set up their traps, the young agents had to be able to use their own bodies if the need arose. First of all the men were ordered to sleep with their girl friends in the large dormitories so that they might lose their inhibitions. Then they were instructed to engage in homosexual affairs with each other.

"This was not intended to make them homosexual, a psychological impossibility," the defector I had interviewed in Bayswater explained, "but merely to widen their sexual horizons, shall we say. If they were invited to an orgy in the West, they had to be able to participate with both sexes. If they thought a Western male could be blackmailed after having an affair with them, then they had to be able to overcome any repugnance they might feel and sleep with him. At all stages of the training it is emphasized that any task which is for the good of the Soviet Union must be undertaken." Demidov recalled that "the students were often distressed during this part of the course, but eventually they overcame their revulsion."

Pistol shooting was another regular part of the training schedule. An extremely sophisticated range, imported from America, enabled the students to practice gunning down targets in a busy street. A film scene would be projected onto the target board and an instructor would indicate the victim. The students then shot him, taking care to miss innocent bystanders. In addition to shooting with normal automatics, the students became experts with silenced gas pistols. "The weapon is about four inches long and is accurate only within a range of twenty-five feet," said Demidov. "But it makes a sound no louder than somebody snapping his fingers; it kills in four seconds. The cause of death is afterwards very hard to establish."

The students are also taught how to kill by using poisons and how to dope victims using drinks, sweets, and cigarettes. They are taught which drugs should be used for different tasks and what symptoms the victim will show. They are also shown which antidotes to take should they themselves be drugged.

After a stringent final examination, successful students are flown to a recreation center in the Caucasian mountains for a month's holiday They then return to Moscow for months of practical training under realistic conditions Occasionally such realism is demanded that an embarrassing encounter ensues. Not long ago, one student was spotted taking pictures near Dzerzhinsky Square by two Soviet militiamen. They immediately arrested him and were dragging him away when a red-faced KGB instructor dashed up and produced his papers. There was a considerable argument on the pavement, watched by some astonished tourists, before the police reluctantly accepted the instructor's documents. It was a black mark against the student's name which must have taken months of hard work to erase.

Not all arrests are accidental. Sudden seizure followed by intensive and often brutal interrogation is the lot of every student. Female as well as male trainees are stripped naked, punched, kicked, and subjected to all manner of humiliation and degradation by skilled KGB investigators. Every word of their cover stories is picked over, checked, and flung back in their faces. One female agent, who defected to the West in the late sixties, told her CIA interrogators that she had been thrown into an ice-cold cell and ordered to remove all her clothes. Then, as she stood nude and shivering on the flagstone floor, uniformed and plain-clothed guards came in and began to insult her. They discussed her body loudly and made her stand with her legs apart while they spat at her. Finally one of the KGB men sent the others away, undid his trousers, and threatened to rape her unless she talked.

A male student suffered equally undignified treatment at the hands of his brother KGB officers. After enduring everything with as much composure as he could muster, and sticking to his cover story doggedly, he was allowed to get dressed.

"Congratulations," said a senior instructor. "Have a cigarette. You've done very well. I am sorry about the rough treatment, but you must be prepared for what may happen if the other side arrests you. By the way," he added casually as he lit the youth's cigarette, "is it the third section training group you belong to?"

"No, the fourth," began the student. The next instant a cracking open-handed blow had crushed the glowing cigarette into his cheek and sent him spinning backwards off the hard wooden seat. "Never relax! Never!" shouted the officer. "I merely hit you, it could have been a bullet."

Among the training manuals which the students study is one written by four KGB staff officers. In 1973 a copy found its way into the hands of the CIA. The brief extracts quoted below give an excellent insight into the aims and techniques which these spy masters of the future are taught. A note at the end of the textbook explains that it has been published "in accordance with the plan for editorial and publishing work of School No. 101, approved by the leadership of the First Chief Directorate of the KGB under the Council of Ministers, USSR. Editor: Colonel A. I. Avdayev. Literary Editor: T. V. Mitrofanova. Senior Proofreader: I. B. Dubenskaya. Copies printed: 100. Duplicated by rotary press at School 101. TOP SECRET."

This book lists the prime targets for the attention of Soviet agents working in the United States. These include the president and his Cabinet, as well as members of the National Security Council (which has overall control of security matters in the United States), the State Department, the Department of Defense, the Central Intelligence Agency, and the Federal Bureau of Investigation. Among the individuals listed are government employees, scientists, economists, engineers, young people who have good prospects of joining the government or companies engaged in military research programs, and civilians attached to centers engaged in classified research.

Agents are taught in the textbook that five factors may be involved in persuading a useful contact to hand over secret information. These are (1) because they are convinced that the Communist way of life is preferable, (2) because they feel sympathy towards the USSR, (3) because they are unhappy with their way of life in the United States due to either government policy or the philosophy of big business, (4) because they are in financial difficulties, or (5) because of some character weakness which becomes apparent "after a close study of their way of life." Such weaknesses are awarded stars according to the importance with which the KGB regards them. A weakness for women ranks second only to greed and gains four out of a possible five stars.

The textbook quotes at length one case in which sexpionage was successfully used to gain information from a security-conscious United Nations employee. For this particular assignment a member of the Soviet Foreign Intelligence Residency who worked in a cover job at the United Nations recruited a raven who is given the code name "Del" in the report.

Del was a Spaniard. "He was out of work at the time of contact," says the author. "He had an interesting appearance with typically sharp Spanish features and enjoyed a great success with women. He was married to a Russian whose parents had left Russia during the Revolution." An economics specialist, he was persuaded to help the Soviet Union for ideological reasons. The residency found him a job on a small magazine, a cover which enabled him to gather minor scraps of intelligence from the UN. Then the Spaniard was given his first major assignment, to seduce a female employee. The report on this case continues, "Having made the acquaintance of the employee, he soon began to live with her." Before long Del had such a powerful hold over the woman's emotions that he was able to recruit her as an agent. At his bidding she changed her job for one which gave greater access to secret information. The subversion was complete when the woman agreed to accept money for her spying. The report concludes, "The Soviet intelligence officer's correct interpretation of Del's personal qualities showed the expediency of acquiring his co-operation and made it possible for the residency to acquire a valuable recruit."

From all of this it is obvious that the KGB's highly trained, tough, and dangerous professional agents are taught from the start of their professional careers that sexpionage is not only a legitimate espionage technique but frequently the cheapest and most effective method of obtaining information.

For the KGB swallows and ravens life is usually a great deal simpler. They merely have to use their bodies in the most effective way possible. The details and outcomes of the operations hold little interest for them, and usually they are provided with only the most minimal of information.

Although these men and women play the role of prostitutes, they would not consider themselves as such. According to Anatoli most of them come from respectable middle-class and professional backgrounds. Many of the ravens have other jobs and only work for the KGB because such a powerful connection can help their careers and make their private lives more comfortable. At the start of their training most of the attractive girl swallows are as innocent as any young schoolgirl. Some are still virgins when they enter the sex schools. Many middle-class Soviet families are very prudish about sex, and sex education in schools is usually evasive. Often the girls have no knowledge of the true nature of the training which lies ahead of them. They have signed on for the course after being dazzled by the prospect of a comfortable apartment and plenty of money with a secure state organization. Even if a few suspect the job may have something to do with espionage, it is doubtful that any of them would walk smiling and enthusiastic across

SECRETS OF THE SEX SCHOOLS

the threshold of their training school if they realized the misery and degradation that lay ahead. There are some extremely unpleasant surprises ahead for every young swallow before she will be allowed to leave her love nest.

4

Confessions of a Swallow

The old, walled, brothel area of the Tunisian city of Sousse was the extraordinary backdrop for an interview I had with a former KGB swallow whom I will call Vera. She was trained at the Verkhonoye House of Love and worked for the KGB for nearly three years in the early sixties. After defecting to the West, she settled in Paris where she married a Tunisian engineer. In 1969 she returned with him to North Africa. Today she lives in a small apartment outside Sousse with her husband and two young daughters.

My meeting with Vera was arranged only after weeks of delicate negotiation, carried out on my behalf by a former member of the German Federal Intelligence Service (BND) who had interrogated her shortly after defection.

At first, Vera, who is now in her mid-thirties, was unwilling to discuss her career as a swallow. She told me she feared being expelled from Tunis if her past became known, and that her disclosures might make her the target of a KGB assassination squad. Eventually, on a guarantee of complete anonymity, she agreed to talk about her training and work in the Soviet Union.

It was Vera who suggested our meeting place, a small café in the brothel area, where scores of prostitutes, many of them old and amazingly ugly, ply their trade from windows and street doors. When I arrived in the late afternoon, trade was slack and, except for a few tourists and the occasional groups of young Tunisian soldiers in shabby khaki, the streets and alleys were deserted. The women sat on wooden chairs in the slanting sunlight, or gossiped across narrow lanes.

After sitting at the café for twenty minutes, I saw a trim middle-aged woman in a brightly colored print dress strolling towards me, apparently oblivious of the glances of the soldiers and the glares of the prostitutes. She introduced herself in strongly accented French and accepted a cup of coffee. For a few minutes we exchanged casual conversation; then she said briskly that the interview should start as she had to get back home early to make her husband's evening meal. After a slight hesitation she agreed that our conversation could be tape-recorded. My first question was why we had met at such an unusual rendezvous; the lounge of a hotel would have been less public and considerably more comfortable.

"I thought we should talk here because it helps me to remember," she explained hesitantly. "Not so much the details but the way it felt to be . . . a prostitute. I was trained at great expense by the Soviet Union to become the bed companion to whichever man those in authority selected for me. When my old German friend first asked me to meet you I refused, as you know. Partly I was frightened for myself and my family. But also I felt unwilling to dredge up memories of a time when I suffered a great deal of mental anguish. I was persuaded that this aspect of the KGB's operations should receive wider publicity. In the past few days I have been trying to remember what happened to me as accurately as I could. Facts were not so hard, I found, although painful to recollect." She hesitated for a long moment. "But I found it impossible to re-experience the sense of deep despair I felt at the life I was forced to live Then I remembered this place." She stared around us. "Here a woman can be bought for about $1.50. At night there are lines of men waiting their turn at every door. These women are sex machines, trapped into a life every bit as hopeless and degrading as mine was. Thanks to God, I was able to escape. I wanted to meet you here so that I could remember what I was and what I might still have been."

In the silence that followed, Vera lit a cigarette, accepted another cup of coffee, then asked, "Now what is it you want to know? Perhaps my background would be of help. You must emphasize that I was not a loose woman, not a sex-hungry teenager. I was brought up strictly by an aunt who was very straight-laced and religious. My father died when I was five years old and my mother had to go out to work to support us Apart from myself there were two brothers, both older We shared a two-bedroom apartment in Leningrad. I was a believer in the party at a very early age and my mother was a dedicated Communist, but my aunt disapproved of all politics I enjoyed school, especially physical recreation. I was a very good runner and received awards. Once I traveled to Moscow with my school athletics team and we performed at a gala function before Nikita Khrushchev.

"Until I was sixteen I had no real idea of what I wanted to do. My strong subject was languages. I used to speak English well, although now I have forgotten a great deal of my vocabulary and find it easier to talk in French.

"My mother wanted me to obtain an office job and so I enrolled in a technical school in Moscow to study the usual secretarial subjects. I stayed in a hostel and enjoyed myself very much. I look back on that time as being especially happy. In those days my hair was dark and, because I had always been careful of my diet and taken exercise, my body was in very good shape. I found that I was attractive to boys and I had a lot of requests for dates, but I refused them all. I was more interested in my work and in athletics. In those days also I was very reserved and inhibited about sex. When the others talked and laughed about it, I would blush and walk away. This was due to the influence of my aunt."

One afternoon Vera was called to see the principal. Sitting in the office was a thick-set middle-aged man whom the principal introduced as a colonel in a government department. The principal told her to answer the man's questions and then left them alone.

Vera continued, "This man started to ask questions about my background and my private life. He listened to my answers casually and just nodded as though he knew everything before I told him. He talked about my father and said he had known him during the war. Then he discussed athletics and commented on the fact that I had been in the children's movement and the Communist Youth League. I said my mother was a good party member, and he said, ''Not your aunt, I hear,'' and laughed He then told me I had been proposed for an important job in the party He said it was a great honor to have had my name put forward, but I would have to work hard to obtain the position. When I asked for more details, he became a little evasive. At least, looking back I feel that he was evasive, but at the time I doubt if I noticed this because I was so excited and proud. I knew it would be a wonderful thing for my mother if I were given this job. I was told it was necesssary I should undergo a medical examination and that this had been arranged in the school medical center for the following morning."

Although Vera had been given regular medical examinations during her school career, this was the most detailed and, for the shy young seventeen year old, the most embarrassing she had ever experienced.

"There were two doctors," she said, "a man and a woman. They paid particular attention to my sex parts and I felt very awkward and ashamed. But it was over at last and I returned to my studies. For more than two months I heard no further news. This disappointed me for I felt I must have failed in some way."

Then Vera received a second summons to the principal's office, where she met the same official as before. "As soon as I came into the room he stood up and took my hand. He was smiling as he said I had been accepted for a final-selection course. Even if I failed, this was a great honor and justified the faith of a large number of people. He explained that I would go to a training school for a four-month-long course. If, at the end, I did not pass the stringent tests, then I would return to the technical school and resume my studies. 'But I am sure you will do well,' he said."

I asked Vera if she realized that the man was a KGB officer recruiting agents. "Perhaps I did," she replied honestly. "He was clearly a man of influence and the principal was distinctly nervous in his presence. However, I was too excited about the prospects before me because he had made it clear that the job, if I was fortunate enough to pass the selection board, would give me a very big salary and an apartment of my own. In addition, he hinted at travel abroad and meeting foreigners."

During the next four months Vera's background was even more closely investigated than before. Nothing disturbing was found and she passed the selection tests with distinction.

"After a few days of holiday with my family, I received a notice telling me to report to a training school outside the city. This was the first thing that caused me some worry because this place had a reputation as being involved with the KGB. Even so, I was too excited to worry about gossip. On May twentieth I said good-by to my mother and left to join the other students in the course. We were driven to the school in a bus which had a uniformed driver. For the first time it really came home to me that I was going to work for the KGB."

The first few days at the school were taken up with lectures on world affairs and party ideology. Vera remembered being told that they were being given the chance to play an important role in the shaping of world history. In return for unquestioning obedience they would receive great material benefits, including passes allowing them to shop at luxury stores reserved for party officials. "When she spoke of these things, the instructress's eyes glowed with excitement," Vera recalled. "But as soon as this instructress had stepped down from the platform, a stout man in uniform got up very quickly and said that while it was true there were material benefits, he was sure it was pure patriotism and love of the party that would be our greatest motivation."

The students stayed at this school for three weeks, receiving mainly political indoctrination. "On one occasion a man in colonel's uniform arrived. He told us he was a staff officer of the KGB and then outlined some of the work which his organization undertook. I remember there was a color film which showed various departments of Dzerzhinsky Square. It was the first time I had realized how large and powerful the Committee of State Security really was."

When this part of the training was completed, the students, fifteen girls and five men, were taken by plane to Kazan and then driven by bus to a complex of buildings standing in large, heavily guarded grounds. This was the Verkhonoye House of Love.

"We were shown into a long two-story brick building which was divided into apartments. Each consisted of a bedroom with its own private bathroom. A big window looked out over a walled garden. It was very clean and comfortable, with simple furniture and fitted closets. Beside the bathroom door, over the dressing table, there was a large mirror. The bathroom itself was much smaller than one would have expected." Soon Vera was to discover that the mirror was a two-way glass and a compartment next to the bathroom contained film cameras. Access to this equipment was via a service door in the passage which had no handle and could only be opened with a special key. At first technicians were very discreet about coming and going to attend to the equipment, but before long these precautions would be quite unnecessary. "We were to learn of the presence of this film equipment in a very terrible way," Vera commented.

Inside the filming compartment the technician was able to change the rolls of 16mm film in two cameras, each covering a different bedroom. Apart from film changes and routine maintenance, the cameras needed no attention and could be switched on or off from a central control panel on the ground floor. This was the setup Vera saw in the early sixties. Today it is probable that TV cameras and video-tape recorders have replaced the film cameras.

"On the first afternoon we were all assembled in a large room in the old building. It had cream walls decorated with pictures of Lenin and

Khrushchev. The girls' ages ranged from about eighteen to twenty-two, I think. Four of the men were in their early twenties, one was about thirty-five. Two of them who appeared about twenty-five were clearly homosexual. The director, a middle-aged man, stood up on a small platform and made a speech of welcome. He warned us that our training would be difficult and we might find some of the orders we were given distasteful at first. This was natural in view of the work for which we were intended; but we should remember that we were soldiers fighting in the front line of a bitter ideological battle. In war soldiers were often ordered to do things which, as individuals, they would find repulsive; but hard sacrifices were essential. Any feelings of repugnance must be thrust aside and we should bear in mind that our work was a sacred duty to the party and to our country.

"Since we had not been told the exact nature of our training or of our future work, this speech naturally made us all very bewildered and rather anxious. One girl even whispered to me that we were obviously to be trained as assassins."

The following morning the girls were divided into three groups and assigned team names. Then they gathered in a theater to watch a sex-education film.

"In Russian schools human reproduction is not dealt with frankly," Vera explained, "and this film went further than anything I had ever seen in my life. Every detail of love-making was shown, including oral sex techniques. By the time it was finished and the lights came on, several of us were bright red with embarrassment. But our instructors, a middle-aged woman in a white coat and her young assistant, were so matter-of-fact and clinical about it all that we soon stopped blushing."

Other films followed, many of them illustrating sexual perversions. During the break for lunch, wine and spirits were served and the girls were invited to drink liberally. Afterwards they all went into a large room.

"The room was arranged with easy chairs set in a circle," Vera told me. "The floor was carpeted. We sat down and waited. The instructress came in and immediately told the girl sitting next to me to stand up and remove her clothes. The girl was very embarrassed, but the woman kept ordering her to undress in a hard voice; so she slipped out of her skirt and blouse, then took off her brassière but kept on her panties. The instructress shouted angrily that she must remove everything. The girl started to cry, but she obeyed. When she was naked she was ordered to walk around the circle so that we could all examine and touch her body. Then she was told to sit down, still naked, with her legs apart. After that another girl was ordered to do the same thing. I felt sick waiting for my turn and when it arrived I thought I was going to die of shame. It was not so much being seen nude—that had happened to me often in school—but the circumstances were so unusual, and being closely studied and touched by the others was so degrading. Finally we were all naked except the instructress.

" 'You have to learn not to be shy about your bodies, which are now weapons to be used in a cause,' she told us.

"Finally we were allowed to dress. Then came a break of about fifteen minutes, followed by another lecture. I forget the subject.

"The following morning the whole group assembled in the large lounge. Once again the chairs were arranged in a circle, but this time there was a mattress on the floor, in the center. A middle-aged male instructor entered, accompanied by a young man and a young woman, both wearing dressing gowns. He told us that we would now see a demonstration of love-making techniques. The couple dropped their robes. Underneath they were completely naked. They went into the center of the circle and started to embrace. The woman rubbed the man until he was aroused and then they lay down on the mattress. The instructor stood close to them and pointed out the techniques the woman was using to stimulate the man and make his sexual response more pronounced and exciting. The woman was told to use her lips and tongue on the man. They did all this without any signs of embarrassment. Finally different positions of intercourse were demonstrated, and the lecture finished with the couple completing their love-making.

"At the end of this we sat in a stunned silence. We had never seen anything like it. I can clearly remember the confusion my mind was left in. I felt excited and aroused to some extent by what I had seen. But more than excitement I felt disgust. I felt I had been exposed to something dirty and debasing."

Vera and her companions were given very little time to contemplate the demonstration. A few moments after the couple had departed, the door opened again and three more male instructors came in.

"My heart stopped beating," Vera told me. "I assumed, and I think several of us did, that we would now be expected to make love in public with these men. Although what happened was bad, it did not turn out to be that bad. We merely repeated the performance of the previous day, each girl undressing in turn, this time before a male and female audience. On this occasion the men kept silent and merely stared at us. They made no attempt to touch us, although we girls were once again instructed to massage one another's bodies. The following morning we undressed again with the men present. This time they touched and caressed us. On the sixth day the men began to abuse us and comment on our bodies. At first it was totally humiliating. During the first week I often cried myself to sleep out of shame. But slowly it didn't seem embarrassing any longer. I was even able to ignore the remarks of the men. However, some girls got angry and answered back equally rudely and they were reprimanded by the instructress."

On the evening of about the eighth day a busload of young officer cadets arrived at the house of love. They were neatly dressed and carefully groomed. Later one of them told Vera that this regular assignment to the sex school was given to the best cadets as a special award.

"Each girl was given a partner for the evening. Mine was a tall, darkhaired man of twenty-two. He told me that he came from Moscow and that his father was also in the army. He was quite good-looking, although his conversation was limited to army matters and shooting, of which he seemed very fond. It was to this stranger that I lost my virginity."

On the ground floor of the sleeping quarters there was a cocktail bar, complete with easy chairs, dim lighting, and a long counter behind which stood a white-coated barman.

"There was every kind of drink you can imagine, and we were told that the soldiers would get us whatever we liked. The instructress said that we must pretend that the men who had been assigned to us were "targets" to be seduced. They would play the part of nervous foreigners. We had to calm their fears and talk them into our beds. Each of us was warned that the tables, at which we would sit, were fitted with microphones. In this way our sales pitch could be monitored and played back to us for comment after the session. I went over to my target and talked to him for five minutes. He offered me a drink. I asked for a gin and tonic because I had never drunk that before. It was a British gin, I remember, and I didn't like the taste.

"The soldiers were only too eager to go off to bed, but they played the part of reluctant Romeos to the best of their ability. They finally allowed us to escort them along the corridor and up a flight of stairs leading to the sleeping quarters.

"We had been told that in the bedrooms we must make love on the coverlets and not under the sheets. I had explained to my soldier that I was a virgin and begged him to be gentle with me. But after the long build-up in the lounge he was too excited. He pulled off his clothes very quickly and was naked almost before I had removed my blouse and skirt. There was no romance for me that evening. He tore off my brassière and began to massage my breasts very hard. He was an animal. It was the first time I had been alone with a man who was so aroused and so virile. I was extremely frightened. He pushed me down onto the bed and flung himself on top of me. I remember that his chest was matted with black hair and that he had beads of sweat on his forehead. Then I felt the pain of his entering me and I cried out. I begged him to be more considerate, but he continued as harshly as before. Then it was over for him and he just flung himself off me and lay back on the coverlet gasping. I went to the bathroom and washed myself. I ached and was trembling from his assault. I started to dress but he pulled me back onto the bed and had sexual contact again."

Vera believed that this first lesson in love had been for her private instruction. That night, when the men had driven back to the barracks, the girls shyly compared notes about their experiences. One confessed that her cadet had been unable to manage anything at all, and Vera thought to herself that the girl was fortunate indeed.

The following morning they all assembled in the theater for a film show. As soon as the first piece of film came up on the screen one of the girls gave a cry of horror. There, in full color and sound, was that girl and her soldier. The camera had a wide-angle lens pointed down onto the bed.

"A terrible silence fell as we watched," Vera told me. "The girl involved had buried her face in her hands and was sobbing loudly. I stared at the screen in fascination, although my instinct was to close my eyes at this dreadful invasion of her most intimate moments. We could hear their chatter and the man's groans; not a detail was lost. Halfway through, a terrible realization struck me. If this girl had been filmed we all must have been. I started to tremble with fear."

After the film the instructress stood up and began to criticize the girl involved for the way she had handled the situation. So sharp and unkind were her comments that the girl became hysterical and, when the instructress had sat down again, she fled outside.

It was an ordeal which every girl had to endure. Vera's room being almost at the end of the corridor placed her nearly last on the list of films.

"When I realized they were working methodically along the corridor, I could calculate how many films would be shown before mine. I knew I had done badly, from the school's point of view, and was fully prepared for the harsh words which were thrown at me. Seeing a film which involved people we knew was much more arousing than watching the sex education and pornographic films that had been shown previously."

After the showing the girls were all very disturbed. Some giggled helplessly, others cried and refused to look at their companions. One girl went around asking everybody if they had noticed what a powerful man her lover had been. She kept saying, "He was more stallion than man."

On three other occasions the girls were provided with partners and ordered to make love before the cameras. The first time this happened, terribly aware of the lens prying on them, most of the girls were very inhibited. "They tried hard to turn themselves into the sort of sex machines which our instructress obviously expected. As a result our partners found love-making with us extremely dull. One girl even received a beating from her partner for 'acting like a robot.'"

These partners were also experienced young men, but on the second occasion the girls were told to seduce teenage boys. "The eldest was about seventeen and the youngest fifteen; none of them had made love to a woman before. They were extremely nervous and didn't know how to behave or react. This was part of our training, to learn how to calm the fears of inexperienced men and make them enjoy their sexual experience with us, so that they would become infatuated. I had a boy of about sixteen, I think. I can remember very little about him except that he was enthusiastic but clumsy and needed a lot of help."

The final partners provided by the house of love were completely the opposite of the gauche boys. They were all men in their sixties from whom a performance had to be skillfully coaxed. "When I had undressed, very sexily in order to try and arouse my white-haired partner, I undressed him. He was not in the slightest bit aroused and I thought it was going to be a failure. Then he confided that he enjoyed being beaten, so although this made me cringe, I thrashed him. After that there was no trouble. When the film was shown the next day some of the girls laughed. But the instructress praised me and said I had learned my lessons well."

The details which Vera gave me about her training sessions contrasted interestingly with information given to Western intelligence in the late sixties by a defector named Dimitri Labyav, who had trained as a raven in the house of love.

As we have seen, girls were trained to make love to a wide range of partners, most of them virile and presentable men. The ravens, however, were taught exclusively to make love to middle-aged women.

"This was because our future targets were most likely to be middle-aged women, unattractive, frustrated and dull," Dimitri explained. "To have sex with a pretty girl is easy, but being passionate to order with a frigid spinster takes skill."

Ravens received lectures on the erogenous zones and watched sex films. Practical sessions, which were filmed through two-way mirrors, all involved middle-aged women. For Dimitri, the instructor selected an ugly, uncouth, and unwashed peasant. "She aroused in me a deep sense of disgust," he admitted. "Yet I forced myself to go through with it, aware that I was being watched through the mirror. The final lesson involved each of us making love to a woman before the rest of the class. The training was designed to turn us into animals capable of satisfying the cravings of any woman."

In Dimitri's instruction group, as in Vera's, were a few males who kept themselves apart from the others and were, as a result, termed "quiet ones." "These men were homosexuals being trained to ensnare homosexual foreigners," Dimitri told his interrogators. "I understand they were young male prostitutes forced into the job against the threat of imprisonment. Some were very young, all were good looking. They seemed to suffer a great deal from the dehumanizing training methods, and two of them committed suicide during my stay there."

In 1965 a former homosexual student at Verkhonoye was instrumental in ensnaring a young attaché at the British Embassy in Moscow, William John Vassall. The official was invited to a party at a KGB apartment and seduced. Seven years later, after his arrest, Vassall told his interrogators, he remembered lying on a couch completely undressed. The Russian officer beside him was naked. Then the lights were switched on and a man took photographs of them. These pictures were used to blackmail Vassall into handing over British Admiralty secrets.

For Vera, the worst part of her swallow training was the way it slowly changed her personality. "I could feel it happening to me yet I seemed powerless to prevent it. It was not simply that I became less inhibited about my body or the sex act, but I felt myself getting harder and more calculating. I no longer saw human relationships as being important. A man was merely a target, to be rapidly assessed and then dealt with. Which approach will be the most effective? How will he perform in bed? How quickly can he be seduced? These were the questions that now automatically entered my mind.

"By the time our training was completed we were hard, cynical, sophisticated young women capable of bedding any heterosexual man and providing him with the time of his life."

Back in Moscow, Vera was given her first assignment. She was told to seduce an American businessman staying in a central-Moscow hotel. "I was given a job in the hotel as a chambermaid on this man's floor. As he was going to stay in Moscow for two weeks there was no great rush. I let him get used to seeing me around. After four days I went into his room at a time when I knew he would be taking a shower. I felt no emotion at all as I pushed open the door to "accidentally" burst in on him. He emerged from behind the shower curtain holding a towel in front of him. I pretended to be very confused, but I made no move to leave the bathroom, and I kept my eyes fixed on the towel. Finally he asked me if I had ever seen a naked man before. I said, 'only my brother, and he is just fourteen.' Then the man laughed and removed the towel. He asked if I noticed much difference. After that it was quite easy. He led me into the bedroom to demonstrate the 'difference' and we made love on the bed. We had just finished when the door burst open and two KGB men came in. They said they were the hotel security men. I started to scream and said the man had raped me. They dragged him off the bed, still somewhat wet, and started to punch him. They told him he was in serious trouble. He begged me to tell them the truth, to admit that I was partly responsible. But I swore it was all his fault. Anyhow, this went on for about five minutes and then, suddenly, they all began to laugh. The American got up and pulled on his clothes, saying to me in Russian that I was very good in bed. It was a final examination and I passed successfully. The KGB wanted to see if I would keep up the pretense of a rape even when the man wept and pleaded with me to tell the truth. The training course had done its work well. Even while I believed that the man was an innocent victim, his whole life now threatened with ruin, I felt no emotion. I felt nothing for him."

Vera was given a comfortable apartment of her own, although while working entrapments she usually set up "home" in one of the more luxurious KGB "swallows' nests." For a time she was willing to endure her way of life in return for the luxuries it brought her. But gradually doubts began to set in. Her association with Westerners gave her a new slant on world affairs. At first she dismissed their stories as propaganda, but gradually she realized that much of her education stressing the abject misery and total corruption of the capitalist system had been false.

"I became sickened by what I had to do," Vera told me. "In 1963 I seduced a young French student whose father had an important position in the mining industry. He was due to marry a girl from a very aristocratic background, and the KGB knew that a scandal would wreck the match. The boy was not really interested in me at first; he loved his girl friend deeply and did not want to be unfaithful to her. But I used all the tricks I had been taught until first he came to trust me and then to lust after me. We went to bed and the pictures were taken. Then the boy was told that the photographs would be sent to his fiancée's family unless he persuaded his father to hand over certain commercial intelligence. I have no idea what it was they wanted. The boy said he needed time to think it over. The same afternoon he walked in front of a car near Red Square and was killed. Perhaps it was an accident." Vera shrugged. "But it was the breaking point for me. I knew I had to get out of my job and that meant leaving the country."

Three months later Vera achieved this by using the techniques she had been so carefully taught at Verkhonoye. She seduced a KGB colonel and persuaded him to give her the documents she needed for a holiday in East Germany. From there she crossed into the West. She was incredibly lucky to live to tell her tale, for few swallows are ever allowed to fly far from the nest. If they try, their wings may be brutally clipped.

In 1968 a German woman, Gudrun Heidel, died instantly when she fell under a speeding car on a West Berlin highway. At first it seemed like a normal automobile fatality. The driver was charged with dangerous driving and fined $200. His protestations that the woman seemed to have "flung herself" under his wheels were not believed by the court. Then detectives investigating the case discovered that pretty Gudrun's passport was false. It gave her name and profession as that of a West

German teacher, but checks revealed that this woman had died of cancer some months earlier. A common Soviet method of providing illegals with identities is to take names from tombstones and, suspecting that this might have happened in the case of Gudrun, the civilian police handed her dossier over to the counterintelligence service. Their agents discovered a number of witnesses who had been on that stretch of highway just prior to the accident and claimed that the twenty-nine-year-old blonde had been walking beside a middle-aged man. One witness said they seemed like father and daughter. The man had not come forward after the accident, but his description fitted that of a fifty-eight-year-old East German agent.

Then came the most astonishing incident of all. A West German lawyer, Herr Jurgen Stange, was approached by an East German colleague named Wolfgang Vogel. Vogel has a spectacular reputation for arranging spy swaps. It was through his wheeling and dealing that Colonel Abel was exchanged for Gary Powers, and Gerald Brooks for Gordon Lonsdale. This time Vogel was in the market for a corpse. He was prepared to exchange two live West German agents for Gudrun's body. At this point an impregnable cloak of secrecy descended on the affair. Vogel has since denied that he offered any such swap, but my own West German sources insist that a deal was arranged and that Gudrun, packed in a crate, was driven across the frontier in the gray light of a January dawn. As her corpse traveled in one direction, two convicted West German spies walked to freedom from the other.

The scenario leading up to Gudrun's death seems to have been as follows. She was a KGB-trained swallow acting under orders from East German intelligence. Her instructions had been to travel to the West as a refugee and then seduce an American officer with access to NATO secrets. At first the plan went faultlessly. Gudrun met the officer at a party and they soon became lovers. But as their relationship developed Gudrun made the worst possible mistake for a swallow—she fell in love with the target. When her spy master ordered her to put pressure on the American she hesitated. If he discovered the truth she might never see him again, so Gudrun kept silent and stalled for time. The East Germans then began to suspect that she had changed sides. A spy master met her and gently probed her reliability. He said she must deliver the goods or face the consequences. Still she refused. The man had his orders. The road, slippery with rain, was almost deserted. The East German's hand came back as though to scratch his ear, and as the car drew near he brought his palm crashing down between her shoulders. Gudrun plunged to her death beneath the screeching tires.

An even more macabre fate overtook Miriam Morales, a KGB sex spy and widow of the Marxist leader in the Dominican Republic, Otto Morales. She worked on sexpionage entrapments in Brussels after her husband was shot by police in the Dominican Republic in 1970.

In 1971, suspicious that she might have become a CIA double agent, the KGB ordered her to return to Moscow for questioning. Miriam went into hiding when she discovered that a man from Department V of the First Chief Directorate had been sent to eliminate her. But against a professional KGB killer the terrified woman stood little chance. She was killed and her death was used as a terrible warning to other swallows who might be tempted to change sides. On December 11, 1971, a Brussels police officer was called to examine a brand-new tartan suitcase found on a doorstep. It contained Miriam's amputated legs. On December 13 her arms and torso were discovered in an identical suitcase left at an office building. Her head was never located.

Vera was a rare and fortunate exception to the rule that when a swallow leaves her nest, she flies as the KGB directs—or she never flies again.

5

Birds of Prey

Living quietly in a Moscow apartment and working as an illegals instructor in the Second Department of the KGB's First Chief Directorate (dealing with espionage in Latin American countries) is a pretty blonde woman who could tell a remarkable story. According to the official record she is dead, her bullet-riddled corpse rotting in an unmarked grave deep inside the Bolivian jungle. In fact, Laura Martínez, the woman who loved and betrayed the Cuban guerrilla leader Che Guevara, is still very much alive. Her case is one of the strangest in the dossiers of Western intelligence, for it shows the extent of the deceit practiced by the swallows in the KGB-directed missions. Che Guevara loved and trusted Laura Martínez, whom he had met in East Berlin. He never lived to learn the terrible truth that his mistress was a KGB agent, reporting back his every secret to Moscow and, eventually, betraying him to the Bolivian authorities on orders from her Soviet masters.

Laura was born on November 19, 1937, in the Argentine. Her father was a German Communist professor named Erich Bunke. Her mother was a Pole, Nadja Bider. Laura's real name was Haydee Tamara Bunke. In 1952 Tamara left South America and went to East Germany to study at the Stalinstadt grammar school and then at the Humboldt University. As a schoolgirl Tamara was a loyal Communist. She was soon spotted as a potential agent for Latin America by the East German secret service, the MfS, which operates in close collaboration with the KGB. Official approaches were made to her while she was at Humboldt University, where she was studying pharmacy, and Tamara gladly accepted the opportunity for a well-paid and interesting job serving the country which she had grown to love. She was trained in undercover work and subversion. Then in 1959, while still at the university, she was summoned to East German secret service headquarters, at the corner of Wilhelm Pieckstrasse and Rosa Luxembourg Platz, to be briefed on her first major mission. She was told that Che Guevara, Fidel Castro's right-hand man, was coming to East Berlin to negotiate a loan for his government through the Cuban National Bank, of which he was president. In order to maintain and strengthen their influence in that area of the world, the KGB required as much high-level intelligence on Cuba, Castro, and Latin America as possible. They therefore ordered the East Germans to try to plant spies close to the Cuban leader. One such agent was Tamara. Her assignment was to make close contact with Che during his visit to East Germany—the closer the better.

Like most young Communists, Tamara was a fervent admirer of the Cuban revolutionaries and especially of Che. When she was presented to Castro's right-hand man, a few hours after Che's aircraft had landed in East Berlin, Tamara's delighted hero-worship was perfectly genuine. Che was told that she was an expert on Latin American affairs and, as she was also an excellent linguist, bilingual in Spanish and German, she would be able to help him in his negotiations.

Tamara was not alone in being delighted by their meeting. Che was as susceptible as most men to a pretty, vivacious young woman. Within a few hours of their first meeting Tamara and Che were friends. Before he flew back to Cuba they had become lovers.

When Tamara reported back to the MfS, her controller was more than satisfied with the fast progress she had made; so was the KGB when the report was duly forwarded to Moscow. They decided that Tamara would benefit from further tuition in espionage and she was flown to Moscow. In 1961 Tamara flew to Cuba and re-established her relationship with Che. Thanks to his influence, she was given a place at the University of Havana; later she joined the Ministry of Education and became an officer in the Cuban Women's Militia. All this time she was passing regular reports back to Moscow.

In 1964 she warned the KGB that Che would soon be leaving Cuba for Latin America in order to spread his creed of revolutionary Marxism and that his most likely choice of country would be Bolivia. Tamara was ordered to move to South America and build up a secure cover for herself in advance of Che's arrival. She was supplied with a false passport which gave her name as Laura Gutierrez Bauer and stated that her father had been Argentinian and her mother German.

She settled in La Paz and registered in the School of Pharmacy at the Universidad Mayor de San Andrés, the leading institute of higher education in Bolivia. Nobody seemed to think her cover story, that she had left Buenos Aires for the more provincial Bolivian university, strange and she was immediately accepted into La Paz society. A journalist, Gonzálo López Muñoz, who knew Laura well, remembers her as "a nice girl, alert and intelligent, rather quiet. She was a bit Bohemian—she lived in a rundown flat and slept on the floor—but went to a few parties. She loved folk music. She never discussed politics, as far as I recall."

Laura only occasionally broke out of this quiet, unobtrusive role. After leaving the university she was given a job in the Bolivian presidential press office, where several of the female secretaries belonged to a crowd which enjoyed nude parties. Laura went along on a number of occasions, although she never enjoyed the sex performances, or drink and nudity, which were their chief ingredients. She went along with the crowd rather than attract attention to herself by a refusal. Her orders from Moscow were clear. She must do nothing to arouse suspicion while she was cautiously building up contacts in La Paz.

In 1966 the KGB ordered Laura to acquire Bolivian citizenship so that she could travel around the country more easily. She did this by marrying a Bolivian, Antonio Martínez. She then immediately divorced him. By the time Che entered Bolivia, in October 1966, Laura had already traveled widely, building up her contacts, and had a list of more than 200 men and women who would join the revolution as soon as it started. Her excuse for these trips into the wild depths of Bolivia was that she wanted to record folk music.

Che arrived in La Paz in November, having traveled by a roundabout route via Prague, Zurich, and Dakar on two false passports. He destroyed both of these immediately on reaching La Paz and was given fresh forged documents by Tamara, who was now operating under the code name Tania. The documents identified Che as an American sociologist engaged in research work. With these skillful forgeries Che was able to reach the first guerrilla camp, established with the help of Tania and the Bolivian Communist party, at a vacant cattle ranch at Mancahuaca, near the oil town of Caniri. At Mancahuaca, Che was joined by other Cubans.

Using the code name of Ramon, Che set about building up his underground army. He established arms dumps, secret camps, training areas, and even an underground field hospital.

Before long the Bolivian authorities were reeling under the well-organized raids of Che's guerrilla army. They hastily organized a counterinsurgency force, armed, financed, and trained largely by America's CIA. Within a matter of months there were 800 specialized jungle fighters counterattacking under the instructions of US Army veterans of the Korean and Vietnam wars. Despite this formidable opposition, Che's army continued to enjoy considerable military and political success. His army was financed by funds supplied from Moscow through the Bolivian Communist party and from such activities as extorting nearly $25,000 from local industrial concerns as the price of being left alone.

Throughout this time Che's dangerous, mobile existence was being shared by Tania, who lived, loved, and fought alongside him. Although Che was making progress, fomenting student riots, attacking and destroying army posts, and working so effectively amongst the tin miners that the government placed the mine area under a state of virtual siege, the Soviet leadership was growing increasingly unhappy about the situation. They began to fear that Che, who was preaching a Castro brand of Marxism which ran counter to their official party policies, might be so successful that Bolivia would come under Castro's control. That could lead to other countries in Latin America, equally ripe for a Guevara-style revolution, eventually falling under the orbit of Havana rather than Moscow. They decided that Che, as an inspiration to young revolutionaries all over the world, was too dangerous to be allowed to continue. So Tania was sent her orders to betray the man she loved and the cause to which she had dedicated so many years of her life.

In the first week of March 1967, Tania made her way through the jungle to one of Che's most important secret camps. Her excuse was that she was guiding two important emissaries from Fidel Castro, the French writer Regis Debray and an Argentinian liaison officer. They arrived at the stronghold to discover that Che had left some weeks earlier on a reconnaissance march with a small group of his men. Tania waited at the camp until March 21, when she could delay no longer. Information was passed to General Juan José Torres, the Bolivian chief of staff, giving details of the key guerrilla camps. It was the beginning of the end for Che. Underground arms and supply dumps were captured and strongholds attacked at their weakest points. Disorganized and confused, the guerrillas' morale collapsed.

On October 8, Che was wounded and captured, later to be shot in cold blood by a Bolivian army sergeant. Tania was reported killed in an ambush soon after her visit to his camp in March. But there was never any positive evidence for this, and the latest information is that she fled the country on another set of forged papers and reached Moscow safely. "Tania la Guerilla," posthumously famous in Havana propaganda, is still very much alive in Moscow—the swallow returned to the nest.*

Although sexpionage operations are carried out on a world-wide basis, it is only in the Soviet Union that the more elaborate entrapments can be organized. Dozens of men and women, and a small fortune in roubles may be invested in a single entrapment if the target is important enough, such as the French ambassador to Moscow, Maurice Dejean, who became the focal point of a complex and, up to a point, successful sexpionage entrapment in the early sixties.

The story, so far as Western intelligence was concerned, began on September 2, 1963, when a group of Soviet artists came to Britain on a goodwill visit. Eleven days after their arrival one of the party, a film writer named Yuri Krotkov, slipped away from their Bayswater hotel, hurried to the nearest British police station, and told a rather skeptical desk sergeant there that he was a Soviet citizen seeking political asylum. The sergeant showed his extremely nervous visitor to a waiting room, placed a policeman on the door, and phoned his superiors. After the best part of an hour had passed, during which Yuri nervously sipped his first cup of British tea, two noncommittal Special Branch officers turned up. They had to establish whether Krotkov was a crank or a genuine defector, and, if a defector, whether he was worth bothering much about.

The Russian, who was known only as a screen writer in the West, told his interrogators that for many years he had worked as a KGB agent and had helped plan and execute major sexpionage operations. He then went on to tell a story so astonishing in its detail, and so alarming in its implications, that the security officers immediately contacted their opposite numbers in France's counterintelligence organization. If what Krotkov was saying were true, then the result of a long and complicated subversion operation had been to compromise the French ambassador to Moscow.

At first the French refused to believe such an improbable report. Maurice Dejean was recalled from the Soviet Union and subjected to a merciless grilling by French counterintelligence. Item by item Krotkov's story checked out. The French ambassador had fallen for a sexpionage

*The real Tania must have been amused when Patty Hearst used her name after being abducted by the SLA on February 4, 1974.

entrapment. The French were satisfied that no breach in security resulted from the affair, and General de Gaulle is said to have dismissed the episode with a shrug of his massive shoulders and the comment: *"Eh bien, Dejean, on couche."** Even so, the entrapment of such a high-ranking diplomat must remain one of the major achievements of KGB sexpionage.

The machinery of the trap was set in motion in June 1956, at Moscow's Moskva Hotel on the Prospekt Manska, during a meeting between Yuri Vasilevich Krotkov and Colonel Leonid Petrovich Kunavin, when the colonel told Krotkov that their next target was to be Maurice Dejean, who had arrived in Moscow with his pretty young wife the previous year.

A cultured and intelligent man, with a knowledge of several languages and the ability to get on well with people, Krotkov had no scruples about using his natural talents in the service of the KGB. In 1970, giving evidence before an American senate committee, Krotkov (who today lives in the United States under the name of George Karlin) admitted that he had used his charms to organize the entrapment of scores of men from many different countries, including Mexico, India, Pakistan, America, France, Germany, and the United Kingdom.

In Yuri Krotkov's defense it can be argued that his whole life had been spent surrounded by KGB men, whom his family regarded, not with the contempt and fear which the majority of ordinary Russians reserves for Chekists, but as friends. His father, a gifted artist, had been one of the few close companions of Lavrenti Beria. When the young Yuri Vasilevich arrived in Moscow in 1946 it seemed entirely natural for him to turn to these influential friends for help in finding an apartment and his first job with Radio Moscow. Later, when Yuri was an established screen writer, it appeared equally reasonable that the KGB should demand a few favors in return. His first job was recruiting suitable swallows from amongst the scores of hopeful young actresses he met during his film work. It was a task for which Yuri discovered he had considerable aptitude.

The first step in Dejean's entrapment was to gain the ambassador's friendship, and Yuri decided that the surest route was through his attractive wife, Marie Claire. He struck up a formal acquaintance with her

---

*"So, Dejean, you sleep around."

easily enough, but developing their occasional meetings into a close relationship required skill and care.

One evening he and a few friends invited Marie Claire and one of her friends to cruise with them on the Khimki Reservoir on the southern outskirts of Moscow. As she stepped aboard, Madame Dejean congratulated Yuri on possessing such a fine cabin cruiser. He brushed aside the compliment by saying it belonged to a friend who owed him a favor. In fact, it was a KGB patrol boat repainted and refurbished for the occasion, and stocked with wines, fruit, and fresh pastries.

By the end of a pleasant evening, Yuri and Marie Claire Dejean were on the best of terms. Other invitations followed and, gradually, Maurice Dejean was drawn into the relationship. The ambassador and his wife were invited to attend a special film première of the ballet *Giselle*. The opening was elaborately staged by the minister of culture, with several members of the Bolshoi Ballet in attendance. At the film show, Yuri introduced Maurice Dejean to a big-breasted, dark-haired divorcée named Lydia Khovanskaya, who was to act as an interpreter. Lydia was a beautiful swallow of charm and great sophistication gained as the wife of a Soviet diplomat.

After this carefully stage-managed encounter, Yuri took great pains to nurture the relationship between Maurice and Lydia. He laid on a lavish banquet in the elegant Praga, a Czech restaurant on Moscow's Arbat Place. While KGB men kept other diners at a respectful distance, Yuri entertained Marie Claire, and Lydia cemented her friendship with the ambassador. It cost the KGB a thousand roubles for the food and wine, but Kunavin agreed that it was money well spent when Yuri reported back to him. Lydia had no doubt that Dejean was greatly attracted to her. Only a little more time and the right circumstances were needed for them to become lovers.

Not long afterwards the KGB organized the removal of Madame Dejean from Moscow by having her invited out for a day in the country; and Yuri hurried around to see Maurice with a request. A friend of his, he explained, was giving an exhibition of his paintings. The man had trained in Paris. He would look on it as a great honor, and Yuri would regard it as a personal favor, if the ambassador could visit the exhibition. Dejean was willing enough to oblige. Also touring the exhibition, by a happy coincidence, was Lydia Khovanskaya. Yuri suddenly found himself called away and Lydia asked Dejean if he would drive her home. He did so, and stayed at her apartment—a luxuriously furnished KGB love nest—for more than two hours. When he left, Yuri was telephoned by the KGB agent in charge of surveillance with the good news. Delightedly he called Kunavin. The entrapment had worked.

In May 1958, the Dejean case took on a new importance when KGB agents in Paris reported that General de Gaulle was likely to be the new French president. Since Dejean was a close friend of de Gaulle's it seemed certain that he would be promoted to a high position in the new French government and so have access to a wide range of secrets. By this time Dejean's affair with Lydia was flourishing and the KGB had obtained a useful selection of photographs, but, in June, Krotkov was called into Kunavin's office for an urgent consultation. He was told that Lydia was no longer considered to be a suitable swallow. A new scenario had been worked out which required that Dejean's mistress should have a husband, and it was well known in embassy circles that Lydia's diplomat-husband had divorced her.

So Lydia was removed from Dejean's life, on the pretext of going to make a film on location, and another swallow moved into the attack. She was a tall, slender actress named Larissa Kronberg-Sobolevskaya. On her KGB dossier was a warning note that she sometimes drank too much and was inclined to lack discipline. But it was also admitted that men found her strong personality and waif-like appearance highly attractive. Dejean proved no exception. Within a few days of their meeting they were lovers, and the surveillance agents reported that this affair was far more torrid than the one with Lydia. Yuri Krotkov breathed a sigh of relief at the news. Having been forced to snatch one swallow from the ambassador's life, he had been worried that it might prove impossible to replace her.

By late June the KGB had decided the moment had come to spring the trap. In this case there was to be no direct confrontation across a set of incriminating photographs. They realized that, confronted by a direct blackmail attempt, the ambassador would report matters to his government and face the consequences. What they had in mind was a far more subtle approach—the construction of a situation in which Dejean would owe the KGB a debt of gratitude.

After a drive in the country Larissa took Dejean back to her KGB swallow's nest at 2 Ananyevski Lane. Like all such apartments this one was set up with a hidden camera and microphones. But on this occasion the equipment was to remain unused.

As Larissa undressed she told Dejean sadly that this would have to be the last time they could be together as her geologist-husband, who had been away on a field trip, was returning the following day. On hearing this Dejean probably decided to make their last afternoon together a memorable one. Outside the apartment door two hefty KGB men, who were cast in the roles of Larissa's outraged husband and sympathetic friend, waited impatiently for the code word. Through the bedroom door they could hear sounds of increasing passion. Then Larissa gasped out the word. They broke the door open and the horrified ambassador found himself confronted by two tough and, apparently, furious Russians. Finally they appeared to calm down and allowed the shaken Dejean to dress.

"Diplomat or not, you will hear more of this," promised the "husband" angrily.

That evening an anxious ambassador confided what had happened to one of the Soviet friends he had made through Yuri Krotkov. He knew that the man was an influential government official but he did not know that Lieutenant General Oleg Gribanov was chief of the Second Directorate and the mastermind who had planned the entire operation. Gribanov listened intently and with apparent sympathy to Dejean's story.

"It will be difficult to do anything," he commented finally. "You must realize, Maurice, the husband has the might of the Soviet law on his side. However, let us see what a little string-pulling will achieve. After all, we must not let the good name of our most popular ambassador be tarnished by a scandal of this nature."

The next day a smiling Gribanov was able to tell Dejean that the "husband" had agreed not to press charges. Dejean was delighted and thanked Gribanov profusely. The KGB was equally pleased. Krotkov was presented with a gold watch and a decoration for his two-years' work. Now that Gribanov and the ambassador shared a dark secret, a very special bond had been formed between them. In their own time the KGB would expect that debt of gratitude to be paid off, with interest.

In the year that followed the KGB used sexpionage techniques in attempts to subvert other members of the French Embassy, and Yuri Krotkov was involved in all major operations. Some were total failures. The smooth-talking Russian spent weeks trying to meet a young woman in the cipher department, but she refused even to see him alone.

A more successful entrapment was mounted against Colonel Louis Guibaud, the air attaché at the embassy. After hidden microphones had disclosed that the colonel and his wife were on bad terms, Yuri dangled a number of beautiful swallows in the Frenchman's path. Eventually he succumbed and went back to the apartment of a blonde and there was photographed. In 1962 the KGB decided to draw in the line and land this fat fish. Colonel Guibaud was invited to KGB headquarters and shown the pictures.

"You have two alternatives, Colonel," said the KGB man grimly. "Co-operate with us or face the disgrace which will inevitably follow our publishing this material."

But for the gallant colonel there was a third choice. He returned to the embassy, put his affairs in order, and then blew out his brains.

Guibaud's death forced Krotkov to make a decision which had been in his mind for some time. The callous disregard for human feelings and a cynical manipulation of men and women which every act of sexpionage involves had been part of Yuri Krotkov's life for so many years that he had never seriously questioned the morality of his work. Once he began to ask himself questions, the doubts piled up. Blaming himself for Colonel Guibaud's death, Yuri knew that he could no longer work for the KGB. But no man or woman retires from the Soviet secret service unless *they* allow it. Krotkov was left with only one option—defection.

As it happened, the Dejean subversion never caused a breach of security. But it could just as easily have turned the most senior French official in Russia into a KGB pawn. It came to light only because Krotkov had a change of heart and managed to defect. Such high-level defections are rare; as equally uncommon must be those occasions when a sexpionage victim plucks up the courage to face a scandal and disgrace, and perhaps even the destruction of his career, by reporting an entrapment to his superiors. All too often the easiest way out must seem to be to co-operate with the KGB. Their demands are usually graded so that relatively innocent classified material is demanded at first. But once in the quicksand of treachery, it is virtually impossible for a sexpionage victim to drag himself free. How many men keep silent and start working as KGB agents each year can never be known, but one educated guess puts the number of these KGB spies in Western Europe and America at around 10,000. This figure, according to Commander Anthony Courtney, a former British Conservative MP and ex-naval intelligence officer, includes at least fifty influential British officials, mostly members of the Foreign Office. He has long advocated an amnesty in Britain for such blackmail victims which would, he asserts, "relieve an unknown number of men and women from an intolerable load of guilt and fear. But much more important, it would spike the Russians' guns. They would realize that many or all of their victims might have become double agents after accepting an amnesty. They could never trust any of them."

Commander Courtney speaks from a position of special knowledge, for he has studied the Soviet techniques both as a professional intelligence officer and from the unenviable standpoint of a sexpionage victim. As a result of a vicious smear campaign launched against him in 1965, Commander Courtney lost his seat in Parliament.

The case of Commander Courtney is important for several reasons. It was the first example that British security officials had of sexpionage being used to discredit, rather than to intimidate and blackmail. It also provides a grim warning of the time lag which can exist between the KGB obtaining compromising material and their putting it to work. Finally, it illustrates how the bureaucratic, compartmentalized structure of the KGB can prove extremely counterproductive. Here an elaborate operation was only partly successful due to a lack of liaison between two departments within the Second Chief Directorate.

It began on August 3, 1965 when the telephone rang in Courtney's London apartment not far from the House of Commons. On the other end of the line was an old friend and fellow MP, John Tilney, who was speaking from his office in Westminster. Awkwardly he asked Anthony Courtney to come and see him on a matter of great urgency. "Ten minutes later," Commander Courtney recalled, "we met in Westminster Hall. His manner was constrained and anxious as he put a buff-colored envelope into my hand. 'Have a look at that. Several members have already received them.'"

Printed on a large sheet of poor-quality glazed paper were six captioned photographs. The sheet was headed, "I am not a Profumo but a story in photographs." As Commander Courtney later put it: "Two of the photographs represented me in company with a woman, or women, in circumstances which plainly indicated intimacy."

Courtney's old friend was not the only recipient of the smear sheets. They had been distributed to MPs, including the then Conservative chief whip, William Whitelaw, the news editor of the *News of the World,* and Commander Courtney's wife. Given the hysteria which still existed in British politics over any hint of a sex scandal—only thirteen months earlier the secretary of state for war, John Profumo, had been forced to re-

SEXPIONAGE

sign because of his association with call girl Christine Keeler (see Chapter Nine)—it was perhaps inevitable that Anthony Courtney should lose his seat in Parliament.

But why should this bluff ex-naval officer, who had done a great deal to foster good relations between the Soviet Union and the United Kingdom, have become caught up in such an operation?

From his youth Anthony Courtney had liked and admired the Russian people. During World War II he was appointed to Moscow as deputy head of the naval mission. After the war, in his job as an export consultant, he paid frequent visits to the Soviet Union and made a number of friends. However, in May 1963, in the light of disclosures made during the Vassall spy trial, he raised questions in the House of Commons about the diplomatic status of certain employees of the Soviet Embassy, and those of Soviet bloc embassies in Britain. He pointed out that the Russian Embassy in Kensington employed twenty chauffeurs, all of whom had diplomatic immunity and some of whom were known to be high-ranking KGB officers. During the reading of his Diplomatic Privileges Bill Commander Courtney also complained that for nine years Britain had been giving diplomatic immunity to the entire families and servants of Soviet bloc officials, enabling the KGB to build up a sizeable army of potential "legals" in the country. "Legals" are spies using diplomatic cover who, if caught, can only be deported.

It was for this assault on the whole basis of their espionage operations in the United Kingdom that Commander Courtney became the victim of a KGB sexpionage attack. Despite two clear warnings to him that his attitude towards diplomatic immunity was making him unpopular in the Soviet Union, the ex-naval officer had no intention of ceasing his broadsides against what he considered to be a major security scandal. The KGB knew that they would be unable to silence the commander except with an operation of this sort.

The material needed by the KGB for the smear part of their campaign was already on file. It had been obtained two years earlier by an attractive swallow named Zinaida Grigorievna Volkova, who had a cover job in the car rental service of the Intourist organization in Moscow's Ukraina Hotel at 2 Kutuzovsky Prospekt.

When Commander Courtney arrived in Moscow on a business trip in 1961, he was suffering from depression and loneliness caused by the death of his wife a few months earlier. The KGB knew about this personal problem and were only too delighted to capitalize on it.

Zinaida was ordered to cultivate a relationship with the commander. Playing the role of an affectionate and deeply sympathetic woman, the attractive Russian managed to win the MP's confidence. Soon their relationship had developed to the point where she went with him to his suite, where they made love. It was during this brief encounter that the photographs were taken. As they were of no immediate value to the KGB, they were filed away with the commander's dossier for possible future use.

In 1965, when it was decided to mount an attack on Commander Courtney, these photographs were removed from the archives. The commander, whose knowledge of KGB procedure is considerable, believes that the sexpionage operation was begun at a meeting attended by six men, five of them Russian, one of them the British double agent and defector Kim Philby, whose story will be told in Chapter Eight.

Present at that conference in a third-floor room at Dzerzhinsky Square would have been the head of the third (United Kingdom, Australia, New Zealand, and Scandinavia) department of the First Chief Directorate; as the senior officer present he would have chaired the meeting. On his right there would have been an officer from Department S of the First Chief Directorate, the department concerned with the training and controlling of illegals; to the chairman's left Dimitri Petrovich, KGB representative from the British section of the Soviet Ministry of Foreign Trade. This organization, which has offices in Highgate, North London, acts as a cover for industrial and commercial espionage on a large scale. The other two Russians would have been a secretary and a clerk from the archives section who had brought with him copies of the Courtney dossier. The decision to launch an attack on the commander having already been taken at a more senior level, the purpose of this meeting was to plan the actual mechanics of the operation.

The comprehensive dossier before each man provided a wealth of personal information about their target and his private life. They knew that the commander's second wife, Elizabeth, had been told by her husband of his brief affair with Zinaida, which had taken place prior to their marriage. Not only had Elizabeth fully understood the situation but she had even met and liked the girl during a visit to Moscow in 1962. Back home in England she wrote to invite Zinaida to stay with them if she came to the UK on holiday.

Zinaida, like the obedient swallow she was, had passed the letter to the KGB, who had copied it. It now formed part of the Courtney file.

The KGB also knew that the commander's marriage was passing through a difficult phase. In 1964, while he was in the Soviet Union on a business trip, Elizabeth had written to tell him she wanted to leave him. Anthony Courtney had been handed the letter when he checked into the National Hotel in Moscow. He had immediately phoned her and persuaded her to change her mind. But that letter, even though it had been sent over in the diplomatic pouch, had been intercepted by the KGB, opened without damage, and then photographed before being delivered. It, too, formed part of the dossier.

As soon as the meeting started Dimitri Petrovich told his colleagues that the commander intended to visit Moscow on a business trip in July. It was then decided to mount the operation against him in two phases. Soon after he arrived in Moscow, he was to be arrested on charges of "activities against the Soviet State," charges that were to be backed up by fabricated evidence. He would be taken straight to the Lubyanka prison and, while he was out of touch with friends and officials, the smear campaign launched. Unable to defend himself, the commander would be disgraced and discredited, making it more difficult for the British government to press for his release. A list of intended recipients for the smear sheet was drawn up including George Wigg, the Labour Party spokesman on security matters, MPs, and the commander's political agent in Harrow.

In early July the Soviet Embassy in London reported that Commander Courtney had applied for a visa, which had been granted. His trip to Russia was scheduled for July 25. This news was received with satisfaction in Dzerzhinsky Square. Everything appeared to be going according to plan.

Shortly before the Houses of Parliament rose for the summer recess, Courtney tabled an Early Day Motion on the Order Paper, which read:

DANGER TO NATIONAL SECURITY. That this House, recognizing the seriousness of the damage caused to the nation by repeated security cases over the past fifteen years, and conscious of the handicap at present imposed on the Security Service by the extraordinary degree of diplomatic immunity accorded to certain foreign embassies which habitually abuse diplomatic privilege for espionage purposes, calls upon Her Majesty's government to review as a matter of urgency existing bilateral arrangements which confer immunities greater than those allowed for by the Vienna Convention on Diplomatic Relations and to re-establish conditions of mutual diplomatic representation with these countries on a basis of strict reciprocity.

His last words to the Prime Minister, Sir Alec Douglas Home, before the House rose, were to ask when the threat of Soviet espionage would be realized. He received no reply.

With his bags packed for a July 25 departure, Commander Courtney's trip received an unexpected setback, something which neither he nor the KGB could have foreseen. On July 22 the entire country, and especially Conservative Members of Parliament, were thrown into confusion by the resignation of Sir Alec Douglas Home from the leadership of the Conservative party. Under the circumstances Commander Courtney felt it impossible for him to make his trip; it did not occur to him to inform the Russians of the cancellation.

At that point the KGB should have called their whole operation off. But such ponderous machinery, once set in motion, is not easy to halt. Unaware that the first part of the campaign had been rendered impossible, the official in charge of the smear campaign released his documents on schedule. By August 3 everybody on the circulation list had received the scurrilous broadsheet, which finished with the intriguing phrase, "To be continued."

If Commander Courtney had been arrested, the story might well have been continued. As it was, he was able to defend himself against the attack and put the British Security Service fully in the picture. Although the smear finished his political career, it was counterproductive in that other MPs and potential sexpionage victims were now alerted to KGB tactics.

It is likely that the Russians had a second objective in their plan to arrest Commander Courtney on a charge of espionage. At that time two of their top agents, Morris and Lona Cohen, known as the Krogers, were serving twenty-year sentences in British jails. A Member of Parliament imprisoned in Russia might well have proved an important enough hostage to make a swap possible.

# 6

Ravens

The sexpionage operation that gave the KGB access to some of West Germany's most closely guarded secrets began with the lonely-hearts column of a Bonn newspaper and a bunch of red roses, and ended when a wretched, hopeless woman hanged herself from a water pipe in her Cologne prison cell.

In the seven years between the red roses and the suicide, a frustrated spinster believed she had discovered love, and a KGB raven looted a wide range of top-secret military information from her. This included details of two NATO exercises, Fallax and Fallax 66, designed to test the combat readiness of the West German armed forces; details of defense preparations by NATO; the minutes of an important NATO conference held in Canada in 1963; and advanced warning of almost every West German counterintelligence operation against Soviet and East German spies.

This espionage coup, one of the most damaging in West Germany's history, began one Saturday afternoon in the summer of 1960, when the front doorbell rang at the apartment of Leonore Heinz. When she cautiously opened the door the thirty-five-year-old secretary at the Bonn Foreign Ministry saw a smartly dressed, middle-aged man on her front step. He was clutching a large bouquet of red roses and seemed curiously ill at ease.

"Fräulein Gottfried," the man began, then broke off, his nervousness apparently turning into acute embarrassment. "Oh, my goodness!" he stammered. "There has been some terrible mistake. I am afraid I have been the victim of a joke." He thrust the flowers in her direction. "Please accept these roses as my apology for such an intrusion."

Fräulein Heinz stared back at him in amazement. Her orderly, dull existence as one of Bonn's many unmarried government employees was sadly lacking in romance, and attractive men who offered bunches of roses at the front door were not an everyday occurrence. She hesitated for a moment.

"Who did you expect to find here? Why have you brought all these lovely roses?"

"It is a long story." From the pocket of his well-cut suit the man produced a calling card. "My name is Heinz Suetterlin. As for the flowers, I intended. . . ." He broke off.

Heinz Suetterlin was soft-spoken, obviously a gentleman and, just as clearly, the victim of some embarrassing misunderstanding. Curiosity and the hint of adventure proved too much for Fräulein Heinz to resist. She opened the door wide. She smiled. "Come in and have some coffee. My name is Leonore Heinz."

Suetterlin told her he was a bachelor and worked as a film cameraman and photographer.

"In the past my job meant that I was never able to settle down long in any one place," he explained. "But now I am living permanently in Bonn. At the age of forty I am trying to find a wife. To be honest with you, I have been answering the lonely-hearts advertisements in the papers. A few days ago I received a reply from a lady who sent me her photograph and gave me this address. I copied it down very carefully, so there can be no mistake. Obviously I am the victim of some kind of joke. It is cruel of people to plan such hoaxes."

Soon their conversation turned to more general topics. The conservative spinster, whose devotion to her work had left little time for her to develop a private life, found herself greatly attracted to Suetterlin. She was astonished, too, at how much she and this stranger had in common. What had started out as a brief talk over coffee lasted all evening and, before Suetterlin left her apartment, they had arranged to meet the following evening for a meal. From that day onwards Leonore Heinz's private life centered around Suetterlin. They went to concerts together and afterwards strolled along the bank of the Rhine in the warm evening air He entertained generously and was always the perfect host. A few weeks after their first meeting they became lovers. In bed and out of it, Suetterlin proved himself to be an experienced man of the world. He was gentle, considerate, yet always masculine. Within six months they had agreed to marry. Leonore Heinz's friends were delighted, if not a little envious.

One man whose pleasure was unqualified sent Suetterlin a large check by way of congratulations. He was a KGB officer named Yevgeny Yevgenevich Runge, a thirty-five-year-old spy master, whose job it was to control a number of illegals operating in West Germany. Suetterlin, a Moscow-trained raven, was one of his best and most successful agents. In January of that year, Runge had briefed Suetterlin in Moscow for an important infiltration assignment in the Federal Republic. "Here are the dossiers of three women," Runge told the raven. "They all have a job with the federal government which allows them access to secret information. Your orders are to bed them and, if possible, talk one of them into marrying you. You will find that the dossiers include detailed information on the likes and dislikes of each, their interests and spare-time activities. Good luck, comrade!"

Suetterlin picked up the dossiers and walked out of Runge's office into the icy gloom of a Moscow winter evening.

The frustrated spinsters of Bonn have long been a source of concern to that country's security services. The sleepy federal capital, dubbed by John le Carré "a small town in Germany," is just that: an attractive provincial German town which, through an accident of politics, has become a capital. The ministries and government departments which have mushroomed in and around Bonn since the early fifties demand an army of secretaries, clerical assistants, receptionists, and switchboard operators, most of whom are women. They come to Bonn attracted by the imagined glamor of government work, only to find their lives revolving around the office and a dreary apartment. By the mid-sixties there were some 25,000 of these bored and frustrated young women. In the view of one West German security expert I talked to, at least half of them were a security risk.

"Some have relatives still living in the East and this lays them open to blackmail and undesirable pressures," the official told me. "But even without this lever, the fact that Bonn is unable to offer the kind of varied and interesting night life that one could find in Berlin, London, or New York means that their social lives are very limited. Many of them come to Bonn in the hope of meeting and marrying important, wealthy men. But they discover that most of the men they meet are already married, and if they show any interest it will mainly be in casual sex. Under these circumstances the opportunities for an attractive, smooth-talking, unattached male to get them into bed are obviously enormous."

Within a few weeks of their marriage Suetterlin had talked his wife

From his youth, Anthony Courtney had liked and admired the Russian people. However, in 1963 the Conservative British MP raised questions in the House of Commons about security risks resulting from the diplomatic immunity of certain Soviet Embassy officials. The price of the politician's frankness was a scurrilous KGB smear campaign and the loss of his seat in Parliament.

For his exertions on behalf of the East German government, Karl Helfmann received more than $25,000 and earned every penny of it. Dubbed the "Red Casanova," Helfmann drove from office to office and bed to bed, extracting secrets with the deftness of a magician producing silk scarves.

Soon after John Vassall was posted to the British Embassy in Moscow, the KGB arranged for him to meet an attractive and intelligent "swallow." When the lonely naval intelligence clerk remained uninterested in the bait, the KGB exchanged her for a "raven." The famous homosexual entrapment that followed was a blow to British security.

While most spies are drab nonentities, men who survive because they look so unremarkable, Hans Helmcke was a flamboyant gangster. With money conned out of two elderly New York sisters, he bought a Berlin brothel and soon realized he could add to his profits by combining prostitution with espionage. Using information gleaned from his brothel, news service, and detective agency, the amazing entrepreneur sold secrets to both East and West.

Manfred Ramminger, wealthy architect and race-car driver, was always in search of adventure. He got just that when a similarly fun-loving friend introduced him to espionage as an employee of the KGB. One of their escapades was to steal a NATO Sidewinder.

A pilot shows the dimensions of the deadly rocket, which Ramminger transported from West Germany to Moscow via wheelbarrow, Maserati, and air-cargo crates labeled "business samples."

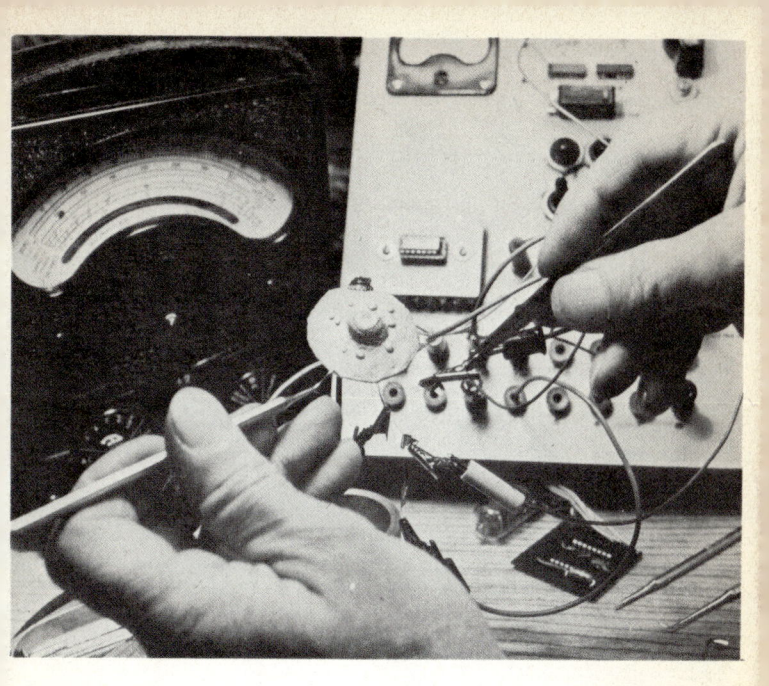

Technology has greased the wheels of modern-day sexpionage. If a female undercover agent wears fake nipples fitted with radio equipment, even the most intimate body search won't reveal that she's wired for sound. Powered by body heat, the nipple's chip transmitter with microphone is said to have a range of several hundred feet.

Lost in the embrace of a beautiful, expertly trained KGB "swallow," a man on business in Moscow is not likely to be thinking about a secret optical fiber tube being used to photograph his fleeting romance.

Sexpionage victims range from world leaders to obscure clerks with access to top-secret files. When Indonesian President Sukarno (*left*) visited Moscow in the early sixties, he was met by the diplomatic smiles of Soviet Premier Nikita Khrushchev. No doubt the smiles continued as night after night beautiful women were directed across the path of the visiting president. But how did Sukarno react when he was escorted to the headquarters of the Russian secret service, the KGB, to see films of his sexual escapades – a prelude to blackmail?

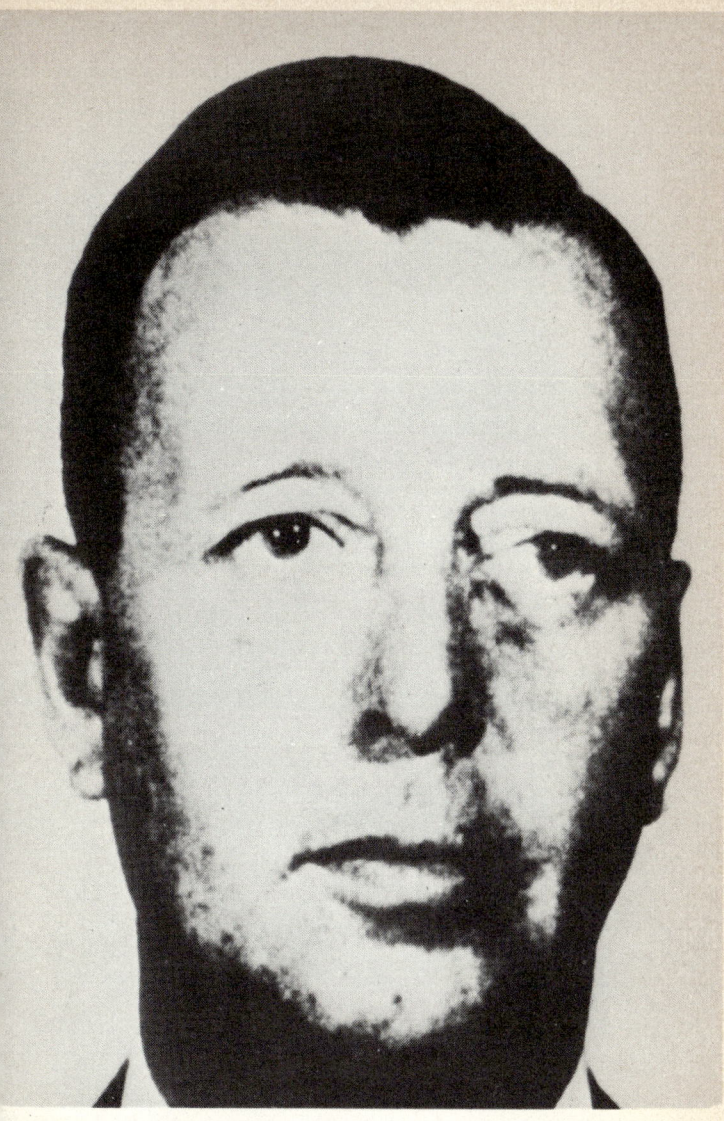

In his job at the Central Intelligence Agency's main European training and operations center, Glen Rohrer was present at hundreds of interviews with spies returning from their missions. He knew the names and cover identities of virtually every CIA agent who passed through the camp, as well as their methods, contacts, and successes. Who could be a more natural target for KGB subversion?

The entrapment of Maurice Dejean, the French ambassador to Moscow, had all the elements of a big-budget movie thriller – a top-ranking diplomat, his pretty wife, a lavish banquet, a charismatic traitor, a yacht stocked with wine and pastries, and a waiflike KGB "swallow" in whose bedroom were a hidden camera and microphones.

into working for the Russians. Exactly what prompted her to bring home the first file of classified documents will never be known. It can hardly have been money. The KGB has never been an especially lavish paymaster, a miserly attitude which is shared by most of the world's secret services, and even when Heinz and Leonore Suetterlin were sending back the vital secret information, they never got more than $250 a week. Leonore's most likely motive was the fear of losing her husband. Obviously a man in his position is able to exert tremendous psychological pressure, and he had been trained by experts in every trick of persuasion and emotional blackmail. Leonore probably removed the first documents only with the greatest reluctance, but having taken classified files once, the subsequent thefts became easier and easier. In the end the Suetterlins had the routine down to a fine art. She would go to work in the foreign ministry carrying a special handbag, provided by the East Germans, which contained a cleverly hidden false compartment. Just before the mid-morning break, she would slip the required documents into the compartment and take them back to her apartment. There Heinz would photograph them with a Leica camera while Leonore prepared their lunch. By the time she had finished cooking, the papers were back in the false compartment and ready to be returned to the files. In all, the Suetterlins were able to steal and photograph more than 3,000 secret documents in this way. Frequently Suetterlin would be given specific instructions about which material the KGB needed. When they wanted to contact him, his special tune—a tango entitled "Moscow Nights"—would be played over Radio Moscow, and the next day he would set out for one of several prearranged "dead drops."

These dead drops are inconspicuous locations where KGB controllers can leave or receive messages. A dead drop or "dead letter drop" may be a hole in a wall, a piece of hollow railing, or a niche in a fallen tree trunk. Suetterlin would collect his instructions and sometimes leave a roll of undeveloped film for collection. When there were no specific instructions, he would tell Leonore, whose KGB code name was "Lola," to steal anything which looked interesting. Of the thousands they took, fifty related specifically to secret NATO subjects and nearly a thousand others were regarded as top secret.

The range of material that the Suetterlins obtained was described thus to Western intelligence by the Suetterlins' controller, Yevgeny Runge, after his defection in 1967:

They copied the personal files of diplomats and functionaries of the foreign service. These provided an ideal starting point for further entrapments or blackmail. Thanks to Lola we in the KGB knew well ahead of time whenever an investigation had been ordered against any of our agents, or agents of the German Democratic Republic by federal German counterintelligence. We received copies of all foreign ministry messages which had to pass across Lola's desk on their way to the coding room. In this way we could study the diplomatic reports from abroad. Often we read them in Moscow before Herr Gerhard Schroeder, the German foreign minister, got a chance to read them in Bonn!

For more than six years the perfectly photographed documents arrived at Dzerzhinsky Square with the regularity of a milk delivery. The KGB gained access to all major NATO and West German defense plans. They discovered the location of secret NATO missile centers and learned details of evacuation plans in the event of a Soviet invasion of Europe. As it happened, some of this material was also reaching them from another source. But no intelligence chief is going to complain about an excess of material, provided he can be sure that the information is accurate and that his agents have not been persuaded to work for the other side and supply him with false intelligence. It was this suspicion which did, eventually, creep into the devious minds of First Chief Directorate officers. Suetterlin and Lola were too efficient for their own good. Doubtful members of the KGB argued that it was not possible that Federal German security could be as incompetent as the Suetterlins made it appear. It took all Yevgeny Runge's powers of persuasion to keep the Suetterlin network in operation.

But the KGB officers were not the only ones having second thoughts. Runge himself was growing increasingly dissatisfied with his work as a spy master and his life as a Soviet citizen. By his skill and dedication he had constructed two major espionage rings in West Germany; in addition to the Suetterlins, he had spies at work in the French Embassy in Bonn. Runge felt that his efforts were insufficiently appreciated. All he got from Moscow for his hard work were complaints and suspicions. While working in the West he had acquired a taste for a different way of life, and he regarded the prospect of eventual retirement on the miserably small KGB pension with horror. In the end it was these worries, coupled with the fear that his superiors might be starting to suspect his loyalty, which caused Runge to defect.

When he fled to the West, Yevgeny Runge was thirty-eight years old. An undistinguished looking man, five feet eight inches tall, with intelligent brown eyes and short curly brown hair, his background provides an interesting insight into the type of men who become KGB spy masters.

Runge was born to German parents in the Ukraine in 1928. After the war he became a Soviet army interpreter and in 1949 joined the intelligence service. Offered the chance of a Western posting as an illegal, he eagerly accepted and was trained for three years from 1952. He was given the false name of Willi Kunt Gast and was provided with a new birthplace, the Pomeranian village of Duninowo, an area which passed from Germany to Poland after 1945. Runge spent two weeks in Duninowo in 1954 in order to familiarize himself with his "childhood surroundings"; then he went for espionage training in Moscow. From there he was sent first to Leipzig, then to Halle in East Germany, and finally to Munich and Frankfurt for advanced training.

In 1956 he married Valentina Rusch, an East German woman who was already working for Soviet intelligence. They were given a thousand dollars and sent to Cologne to establish a dry-cleaning shop as a cover for their operations. But the capital supplied by the KGB proved insufficient for a business of this kind and a few months later, with permission from Moscow, "Gast" set himself up as a vending-machine salesman. As a Soviet agent he was paid $350 a month, money which he banked. His legitimate business was going well enough to support his wife and their son Andrei, who had been born in 1960.

His first assignment was to set up a network inside the French Embassy in Bonn. He achieved this by subverting Leopold Pieschel, a janitor at the embassy, and Pieschel's brother-in-law, forty-one-year-old Martin Marggraf, a free-lance waiter. It proved an ideal setup. The Pieschels were provided with photographic and tape equipment which enabled them to copy secret documents and make recordings of important meetings. Marggraf was trained in room-bugging and given the necessary electronic equipment to wire up hotel bedrooms and conference rooms. In 1965 he achieved a recording coup which must be unique in KGB archives—the pillow-talk of the Queen of England. In May of that year he was working at the luxurious Petersburg Hotel on the Rhine. As one of a select group of waiters screened by the German government to serve at state banquets and official receptions, Marggraf was given the job of waiting on Queen Elizabeth and the Duke of Edinburgh when they stayed at the hotel during their tour of West Germany. He planted a bug, smaller than a matchbox, behind the headboard of the royal double bed. How much value this recording was to the KGB, and what was actually picked up by the hidden radio-microphone, will probably never be known.

Soon after establishing the Suetterlin network, Runge moved with his wife and son into a comfortable house outside Frankfurt and invested some of the legitimate profits from his vending-machine business in a tavern and a company making slot machines and juke boxes.

When suspicions over the Suetterlins' reliability had reached a point where Runge felt obliged to fly to Moscow and talk directly to his superiors, he was ordered to bring his wife and family with him. This was an ominous sign. If the KGB were starting to doubt his reliability, they might intend to hold his family in Russia as hostages. Runge had lengthy discussions with his superiors about the reliability of the Suetterlins and finally dulled the edges of their suspicions. But at Dzerzhinsky Square he saw and heard little to reassure him about his own future. The Moscow meetings came to an end and Runge took his family for a short holiday at the Black Sea resort of Gelendzhik. It was there that they made up their mind to defect.

Back in Moscow, Runge took the precaution of photocopying his personal file so that he could prove his importance to Western intelligence. At this point the KGB suggested that it might be wiser for Valentina and Andrei to remain behind in Moscow, the one move which Runge had been dreading. Runge moved quickly and audaciously by appealing to the head of the KGB, Yuri Andropov himself. Granted an interview, he argued that to return to the West without his family must inevitably arouse suspicions; questions might be asked and inquiries made, which could jeopardize his whole assignment. Andropov agreed and ordered that the family should be allowed to return to Frankfurt. A few days later Runge defected. The spies whose betrayal was the price of freedom were all arrested and put on trial. Suetterlin was given a seven-year sentence; Marggraf and Pieschel went down for three-year terms.

Runge testified that during their years as KGB agents the Suetterlins had supplied Moscow with 969 documents classified as top secret. When he was arrested, Heinz Suetterlin had twenty-three rolls of undeveloped film in his possession. Processed, they were all found to contain secret information. Although the evidence against him was overwhelming, Leonore, at first, refused to say anything that might incriminate her husband. She preferred to take the entire blame on herself. Then she was shown her husband's statement. In it he said bluntly that he had never loved, or even liked, her and that their meeting, courtship, and marriage had all taken place on orders from 2 Dzerzhinsky Square. Even when they were making love, his passion had been no more than an expression of his duty as a KGB raven.

Up to that point Leonore had seemed to be the tougher of the two. Even as she read the devastating document, not a flicker of expression crossed her face. But that evening, four days after her arrest, Leonore removed the cord from her dressing gown and hung herself. When prison officers arrived on the scene she was already dead.

Suetterlin should consider himself fortunate that he was only given three women to seduce. Another successful raven named Karl Helfmann, who was dubbed the "Red Casanova" by federal German counterintelligence officers, had so many frustrated secretaries to satisfy that when security finally pounced and snapped cuffs onto his wrists, the dapper spy only muttered, "Thank God, now I am safe from those women!"

For nearly five years Karl Helfmann had driven all over Germany from office to office and bed to bed. He courted briefly, fornicated expertly, and extracted secrets with the deft charm of a magician producing silk scarves. For his exertions on behalf of East German intelligence, Helfmann received more than $25,000 and earned every penny of it. When he was not courting a new source of secrets, or bedding a regular one, Helfmann was behind the wheel of his Volkswagen. He drove thousands of kilometers a year between double beds, and was on the move so frequently that the East Germans fitted a two-way radio inside his car, to enable him to receive orders and radio his secrets to the East without slowing down. It would have been an exhausting routine for any raven, but for Helfmann the strain must have been especially telling. He was sixty years old.

Before he became a spy for the German Democratic Republic in the mid-fifities, Helfmann had followed a variety of careers. Born in Germany, he trained as a fitter and then went to work in Turkey as an engineer. He married there and returned home shortly before World War II after his marriage broke up. For a time he sold women's underwear from door to door. Then the war came and he got a job in the Junkers aircraft factory, supervising the apprentice workshop. During the war he married again, but this marriage lasted only two years.

In the economic gloom of postwar Germany, Helfmann was hard-pressed to earn a living at all; he traveled around as a tinker, mending pots and pans. His luck changed when he invented a gluing machine. With the money this produced he married for a third time and opened a travel agency in Rudesheim. But his business and his marriage soon foundered. He then started up as a wine exporter and it was this apparently innocent occupation which finally led him into spying. In 1953, he traveled to East Germany to attend the Leipzig trade fair, the premier meeting place of the espionage business. At the fair he met an East German, Werner Brandt, who was overtly a trade official with the East German Ministry of Commerce. In fact, he was a recruiting officer for East German intelligence. Brandt made Helfmann an offer he could hardly refuse. His wine business was turning distinctly sour, and Leipzig was his last hope of saving it from bankruptcy. Brandt, who was well aware of this, told Helfmann he could ensure him profitable orders for his wines in East Germany. In return Helfmann would have to provide general information about the West German economy. The material Brandt required at first was fairly innocent; indeed, much of it could be obtained from documents on open sale in the West. Helfmann agreed without even giving the proposition much thought.

For the next few months he traveled around the Ruhr, buying city-street maps and magazines on economic and business matters, research papers on various industries, and a wide range of similarly innocuous documents. The East Germans paid him well, which encouraged him to co-operate further. After a life of hard work and disappointment, Helfmann must have thought he had found a crock of gold.

He began to drop in at various government and private offices on different pretexts and to flirt with the secretaries. Although he was no Romeo, Helfmann had an attractive personality, being both charming and sophisticated, and he always dressed immaculately. To young secretaries he played first the role of a sympathetic father figure, and then that of a mature lover. It was a performance for which three marriages and innumerable girl friends had prepared him perfectly. Older secretaries were delighted to be courted by such a considerate suitor. For every woman there would be a bunch of flowers, a box of chocolates, or some other small token of his affection. Lunch or dinner would follow, with a romp in bed to set the seal on a perfect day. His regular visits were the high spot of the week for secretaries from Hamburg to Hanover, from Bonn to Bremen.

Not all his informants were also his sleeping partners, however. Many women found his fatherly approach, his generosity, and cultured companionship sufficient recompense for the secrets they handed over. Once a woman was snared she would be persuaded to provide Helfmann with a few items of confidential information, and then a little more. It wasn't really espionage, he would assure her, just some inside information to oil the commercial wheels of his private business. Once they had started to provide him with secrets, Helfmann's demands increased until the women were extracting classified or confidential documents for him to photograph. Often he would take the pictures in their offices, using a 16mm Minox camera. Then he cheekily sent the films for developing to any ordinary photographic dealer, as though they were innocent family snaps.

Racing frenziedly around the Federal Republic in his car, receiving orders and transmitting information over his hidden radio, the Red Casanova led an exhausting, nerve-wracking life. Not only did he have to keep one step ahead of the German counterintelligence, but he also had to make sure his girl friends never found out about one another. At one stage in his sexpionage career he was making love to up to eight different women scattered around Germany every single week. Helfmann had doting informants in the West German Foreign Office who provided state secrets from the files, a love-stricken young woman in the Wiesbaden office of the United States scientific research division who gave him technical secrets, starry-eyed secretaries in aircraft factories who plied him with production details of new developments, and an admirer in the Mannesman steel combine who gave him economic and industrial secrets.

From one of his most ardent girl friends, forty-four-year-old Irmgard Roemer, Helfmann received copies of all the messages passing between the German government and their ambassador in the Vatican. This enabled the East Germans and through them, the KGB, to monitor Western attitudes towards the suspension and arrest of the Polish primate Cardinal Stefan Wyszinski in September 1953. Irmgard, who deserted her husband and two children to work for Helfmann, admitted she was madly in love with him. But she also gave the court a more unusual reason for spying for him. "I helped Karl under the influence of some occult force," she told an astonished judge. "It was as though someone sat beside me and said, 'You must help Helfmann.' "

It was an amazing performance for any agent, let alone a man of Helfmann's age. Not only did he keep his professional mistresses satisfied, but he spent most of the money the East Germans gave him living it up at exclusive holiday resorts. He always stayed at the best hotels, and he always booked a double room in which to entertain his current girl friend.

Just how Helfmann's espionage network came to the attention of the security services has never been disclosed. It is believed that one of his regular sleeping partners saw him on a Mediterranean beach with his latest mistress and became jealous. A telephone call to counterintelligence was her revenge. Helfmann made no attempt to protest his innocence; the evidence against him was overwhelming. But he did try to mitigate the offense by pleading that he had spied for ideological reasons. The court was unimpressed and sentenced him to nearly five years of hard labor. Irmgard was given three years of hard labor and another of his girl friends, a dazzling blonde named Elfriede Buechner, got nine months. As he was led away to start his sentence Helfmann, a Casanova to the last, remarked that the enforced celibacy would at least give him a chance to get his breath back. "You see, as soon as I am released I intend to marry again," he said.

In the cases we have examined so far, the entrapments have been straightforward. A usefully placed woman is seduced and then emotional pressure, rather than threats of disclosure, is used to blackmail her into compliance. But there are other ways in which the KGB uses ravens. A woman may be seduced and compromising photographs taken in order to subvert a third person, such as her husband or her father.

Born in France in 1907 of working-class parents, his father a wheelwright, Eugène Rousseau rose to become a spy master in France's secret service, the SDECE.

Rousseau joined the army as a youth and by 1939 had attained the rank of captain. After the armistice he left the army and became a clerk in the institute of statistics. His knowledge of statistical research led to a job with the newly formed Direction Générale des Études et Recherches, which later became part of the SDECE.

In the early fifties he was posted to Belgrade with responsibility for co-ordinating French espionage activities in Yugoslavia. His cover as secretary to the military attaché gave him diplomatic immunity, and he felt secure enough to bring his family with him. His first wife had died during the war, leaving him with six children to bring up. After the war he remarried and had two more children by his second wife. In Belgrade his eldest daughter, sixteen-year-old Monique, was taken onto the embassy payroll as his secretary.

Yugoslav counterintelligence soon became aware of Rousseau's real task and, with the help of the KGB, set up a sexpionage operation. The Frenchman's dossier was flown to Belgrade by a KGB officer who worked out details of the entrapment with his opposite number in the Yugoslavian intelligence service. After a close study of the documents, it was decided that Rousseau would prove impossible to bribe and hard to blackmail. The fifty-year-old spy was too honest for the first and too cautious for the latter. But his daughter Monique, the KGB man pointed out, was young, innocent, and attractive. It would be easy enough to compromise her and, through her, put pressure on the father. The raven selected for the task of seducing the sixteen-year-old girl was a handsome gypsy boy who had received lessons in subversion techniques from Yugoslavian intelligence. A meeting between Monique and the gypsy was easily arranged and according to a French intelligence report they soon became lovers. Monique was a virgin and as her inadequate sex education had not included any advice about contraception, she became pregnant. Terrified of her father's reaction, she begged the boy to help her. He obliged and, on the pretext of going away for a short holiday, Monique entered a clinic. She had no idea that everything that happened, including the smoothly organized abortion, was part of a KGB-controlled sexpionage operation.

In the boy's apartment was a two-way mirror and hidden camera. Monique was photographed making love and later, at the clinic, having her abortion. The pictures were then used to blackmail her into spying for the Yugoslavs, passing on the secrets which she gained while acting as her father's secretary. Pressure was also put on Monsieur Rousseau in order to make him turn traitor.

The French security service remained unaware of the sexpionage coup. It was only in the late sixties after a Yugoslavian intelligence agent defected to the West, gave himself up to the Americans, and was flown to Washington, that the treachery became known. There, during one of the lengthy interrogation sessions, he mentioned the case of Monique and Eugène.

The CIA passed this information to the SDECE, who put one of their most experienced security officers, Captain André Camus, on the case. For several weeks he had Rousseau followed and his phones tapped in the hope of discovering further evidence, but with no result. Camus then flew to Los Angeles to help the FBI interview Monique, who had married an American pastry-cook and was now a US citizen. She is said to have admitted the entrapment and apparently confessed that she had passed on secret information to Yugoslavian intelligence as the price of silence.

As a foreign national and since the crime had been committed ten years earlier, she could have made such a confession without fear of arrest. But she strongly denied that her father had been involved. Camus was not satisfied. He returned to Paris and had Rousseau arrested. He was taken to SDECE headquarters in the north of Paris, dubbed the *Piscine*, or "swimming pool," by the French. Rousseau's interrogation was undoubtedly harsh.

After thirty-eight hours of continual cross-examination, Rousseau signed a confession. He admitted having been blackmailed into treason. He said he had handed the Yugoslavs secret information and provided the Communists with more classified information later in his career while acting as French ambassador in Algeria. Camus, pleased with the confession, allowed Rousseau to return home under escort. The next morning, however, Rousseau returned to SDECE headquarters and retracted his confession. From that moment onwards he insisted he was completely innocent of all the charges. A secret court thought otherwise. On April 21, 1970, he was sentenced to fifteen years in prison. From his cell in the special quarter of Melun prison, sixty-three-year-old Rousseau began to campaign for a re-trial. Every one of the 286 letters he sent out of prison was a protest of innocence. Influential Frenchmen, journalists, and lawyers began to take notice of the case. The author Gilles Perrault wrote a book, *L'Erreur (The Error)* which criticized the treatment Rousseau had received at the hands of the SDECE and powerfully argued his innocence of the charges. A few days before Christmas 1971, President Pompidou bowed to the weight of public opinion and ordered Rousseau's release.

Whether or not the original entrapment succeeded in turning Rousseau into a traitor, it certainly gave the KGB access to secret information through his daughter. It also ended up by destroying and disgracing a man who may never have been other than the loyal servant of his nation.

Not all sexpionage operations carried out by ravens are heterosexual, and the activities of the "quiet ones" whom Vera saw at the Verkhonoye House of Love are of great concern to Western security.

The most publicized homosexual entrapment was the subversion of John Vassall in 1955. Vassall, who worked as a naval-intelligence clerk, had been posted to the British Embassy in Moscow two years earlier. An introverted and vain individual, Vassall found himself isolated and lonely in the class-conscious embassy. Within a few days of his arrival in Russia, Vassall was under scrutiny by the KGB; a month after his arrival the young clerk was invited to a restaurant and introduced to an attractive and intelligent swallow. When he remained uninterested in the bait, the KGB exchanged her for a raven. This time they were successful. The entrapment was delayed, however, until Vassall's second winter in Moscow, by which time the KGB must have felt he had settled into his job and gained the confidence of his superiors.

A male Russian friend whom Vassall knew and trusted invited him to a party at the Hotel Berlin. It was held in a luxuriously furnished private room. During dinner it is probable that Vassall's wine was drugged. In any event he became unwell and confused. One of the guests suggested that he lie down, and led him to a divan in a curtained recess. He undressed when requested to do so. In his biography he described what happened next: "I was lying on the bed naked, and as far as I can recollect there were three or four other men on the bed with me." He saw that photographs were being taken but, when he returned to the embassy, felt too embarrassed to report the affair. The KGB now had some useful blackmail evidence, but they decided to make completely certain of the subversion by setting up a second entrapment. On March 19, 1955, he accepted an invitation to visit the apartment of a military officer who was on leave in Moscow. The way he describes what happened during their meeting makes it sound like pure soap opera: "He looked into my eyes and grasped my hands. He was a tall man, very quiet, gentle but firm as he held me in his grip. . . . How was it to happen? Would his eyes give me the signal or would we be overwhelmed by the desire to kiss one another?"

Their love-making was interrupted by the arrival of KGB men. The officer dressed hastily and vanished without a word. Vassall found himself confronted by two polite and friendly Russians. They made no attempt to threaten or browbeat him. Once again their understanding of the victim's psychological state was perfect. Vassall was terrified and to frighten him further might have driven him into the arms of British counterintelligence or forced him to suicide.

They showed him photographs taken at the party; they knew about his every move since arriving in Moscow and warned him that he had committed a serious offense under Soviet law. Their victim was hooked and landed. With only very little further pressure, the foolish but previously loyal Englishman was transformed into a very effective Soviet spy.

In Moscow he handed the KGB copies of secret signals that passed across his desk. When he returned to England, in 1956, Vassall became even more valuable to the Soviets after accepting a new job in the office of the Director of Naval Intelligence. He worked from an imposing building in Horse Guard's Parade, not far from Buckingham Palace. From his window he could look down on the garden of the Prime Minister's official residence at Number 10 Downing Street. Both literally and symbolically he was now installed in one of the control rooms of the Establishment's powerhouse. For a spy, that rather drab, cream-walled room must have seemed like the promised land. Every desk drawer, cupboard, and filing cabinet bulged with classified material—secrets Vassall later described as "so hot they could not be sent out of the Naval Intelligence Division at all."

In 1958, the young clerk was promoted again, to the post of assistant private secretary to the new Civil Lord of the Admiralty, the Honorable Thomas Galbraith. By this change of work Vassall gained access to classified information dealing with submarine warfare and the latest research into sonar detection methods being developed at the Admiralty's Underwater Weapons Research Establishment at Portland. In 1961, a major KGB network was discovered operating around this base, and Vassall was ordered to halt his spying activities until things returned to normal. With the exception of this short period, he was an active KGB agent for more than six years. He might have continued spying for the Russians for much longer except for information from a KGB defector. This man warned the CIA that a steady flow of high-level British naval intelligence was reaching 2 Dzerzhinsky Square. The investigations that followed soon traced the leak to Vassall, who was living far beyond his salary. He was arrested in September 1962 as he left his office to collect some foreign currency for a proposed Italian holiday. Found guilty of espionage, he was sentenced to eighteen years imprisonment, of which he served ten. Released on parole in 1972, Vassall talked publicly for the first time about the entrapment and must have echoed the sentiments of many sexpionage victims when he said, "It was like a spider's web. It was done very, very cleverly. At no time could I have escaped. I just got more and more entangled."

Many have charged the Security Service with incompetence for giving Vassall a positive clearance to handle secret information when he made little secret of his homosexuality. The truth is that they were aware of his homosexuality and nervous that he might pose a security risk. But the doubts expressed by counterintelligence men were over-ridden by an entry on his "positive vetting card." It read, "This man is a homosexual but completely trustworthy. I personally vouch for him." The signature was *very* impressive.

In Vassall's case the compromising pictures were used immediately because he was in a position to supply secret information. But such material may be kept on file for months or even years until an opportune moment arises. In the case of another homosexual entrapment, the KGB held their cards for more than eight years.

In 1963, an Italian student, the nineteen-year-old son of a government official, visited the Soviet Union on vacation. He was a bisexual youth, as content to sleep with a pretty boy as with an attractive girl. The KGB provided him with a blond sixteen-year-old boy, and they had sex on a number of occasions. Compromising photographs were taken.

As the KGB had anticipated, the Italian's education and family connections ensured him a job in politics. He joined the diplomatic service and rose rapidly through the ranks. By the time he was twenty-seven he was happily married with a small son. It was then that the blackmail was applied. The young man stood to lose everything by disclosure: his promising career, the respect of his highly conservative family, his wife and son. But despite all the risks the proud young Italian refused to be subverted. He told the authorities and the matter was discreetly hushed up. It is not impossible that Mafia help was requested. Whatever the forces at work, the threat was removed and the man's private and professional future safeguarded. He was lucky. Others, lacking his courage, wealth, and influence, might have turned traitor rather than face probable disgrace.

7

Brothels and Blue Films

At 8:20 on the morning of August 21, 1973, a police patrolman discovered a hideously mutilated corpse lying among some bushes just off the Hamburg-Luebeck Autobahn. The legs had been burnt down to black stumps, the torso was severely charred and the features disfigured. Despite the horrifying injuries, it proved possible to make a rapid identification from police records. The dead man was Hans Albert Heinrich Helmcke, a fifty-six-year-old Berlin brothel keeper, private detective, free-lance journalist, and gangster. Within an hour of the body being discovered telephones were ringing urgently in the headquarters of the BND and BfV, as federal security men tried to establish one crucial fact. Was a branch of Western intelligence responsible for Helmcke's elimination, or had the culprits come from the East?

In the end it turned out that Helmcke had not been the victim of a SMERSH-style execution. He had, in fact, been killed by men from the other twilight world in which he lived and worked, the criminal underworld. But federal security officers had every reason to suspect their own colleagues or a killer from East Germany. Both East and West had motives for wanting to silence this cigar-chewing German who boasted that he was a man with six lives: a reference to the numerous professions he followed. He was certainly a man with a thousand deadly secrets and as many enemies. Of all the men and women I encountered in my investigation of sexpionage Hans Helmcke was the most improbable and the most colorful.

Improbable because, when most spies are drab nonentities, men who survive because they look so unremarkable, Helmcke could never appear other than a flamboyant gangster. His training ground for spying had been the black market and the back alley. He traded secrets just as, after the war, he had dealt in fruit, tinned meat, and chocolate. Superficially charming, Helmcke was a smooth-talking confidence trickster for whom violence was a legitimate business practice.

"Hans would try to get what he wanted by sweet-talking, flattery, and then a bribe," a close associate told me. "But if these failed then he was completely ruthless—the cosh and the gun were the tools of his trade. Not that he used them himself; he preferred to hire mobsters rather than risk his neck or dirty his hands."

I first met Helmcke in January 1965, soon after his fashionable brothel, the Pension Clausewitz at 4 Clausewitz Strasse, off West Berlin's bustling Kurfürstendamm, had been raided by police for the second time. The neatly printed, golden yellow hotel business cards gave no indication that the Pension Clausewitz was a brothel and the nerve center of a spy ring. In fact, its tradition of mingling sex with espionage stretched back to the Third Reich. Joseph Paul Goebbels originally set up the pension as a high-class brothel for visiting politicians, diplomats, and industrialists. He spared no expense to ensure that his guests had a good time, and his girls were said to be the most beautiful in Germany. But Goebbels was interested in more than the entertainment of his visitors. In each room there were hidden microphones connected to a recording machine manned by Gestapo agents in the basement. Even when the pension's VIP lovers concentrated on sex and refused to allow the well-trained prostitute spies to wheedle secrets out of them, the recordings could still be used as the basis for blackmail. After the war the pension closed down as a brothel for a few months, and then re-opened catering to Allied soldiers. So when Helmcke took over the pension he saw no reason not to continue in the tradition of giving sex and espionage services. Unlike Dr. Goebbels, Helmcke had no political motives behind his spying. His only creed was greed.

Hans Helmcke was born on July 4, 1917, in Cuxhaven, a busy North Sea port on the Elbe estuary. His parents ran a food store, but Hans had little interest in the business. When war came he volunteered for the paratroop regiment. In 1945, bomb-shattered Cuxhaven was a city where a man with a dishonest turn of mind could make himself rich, a situation which suited the quick-witted Helmcke perfectly. Working at his parents' food store, which had survived the air raids, he was doing more trade under the counter than across it. A former customer told me, "Hans was able to get hold of any type of food you asked for: fresh fruit, meat, eggs. Even in the worst days of the rationing there was no need to go short provided you had the money to pay his prices."

Hans used his profits to buy black-market furs and jewelry. He was completely ruthless. In 1947, one of his employees, Heinrich Kirsch, tried to double-cross him over a shipment of meat. A few days after their argument, Heinrich was found sprawled out on the concrete path beneath the window of a hotel bedroom in the Black Forest, dead from a fractured skull.

As the economic situation eased in Germany, Helmcke, knowing that the police were on his track, decided to leave the country. In November 1953 Helmcke sailed for New York.

He soon found the way of life so much to his taste that he applied for American citizenship. But his application was refused and, with funds running low, Helmcke began to slip down the social ladder. His expensive apartment was exchanged for a cheaper one, then a sordid room in a West Harlem tenement. By 1954 he was reduced to washing dishes at an all-night café. One story says that he spent a spell in prison after killing a man in a fight. Certainly he was known to the New York police because he twice tried to pay his rent with a forged check.

His luck turned in 1955 when he met two elderly, wealthy German-American sisters, Johanna Wetjen, 84, and Emma Gelhaar, 79, who shared a house in the New York borough of Queens. Helmcke discovered that their maiden name had been Hein. His own mother's name had been Hayn. On this tissue-thin foundation the smooth-talking Hans persuaded the women that he must be a long-lost nephew. He borrowed money from them and eventually persuaded them to return to Germany with him. In January 1960, Frau Gelhaar died and Johanna, to whom she had left her money, made Helmcke her sole heir. A few months later Johanna, too, died and Helmcke, from near penury, inherited in excess of $55,000.

In 1961, Helmcke and his mistress left for Berlin and purchased the Pension Clausewitz.

When he took it over, the Clausewitz had been a moderately prosperous and legitimate hotel. Helmcke completely redesigned the interior, fitting up a luxurious central bar with deep leather chairs and soft pink lights. The mood was one of sophisticated elegance, and the girls were the pick of Berlin's prostitutes. Many of them were amateurs, housewives who liked to earn extra money while their husbands were at work.

"They would say they were going to play bridge or have coffee in the afternoon with friends," a police officer explained, "but really they were sleeping around for cash."

Soon the Helmcke combination of beautiful girls and comfortably discreet surroundings was attracting leading West Berlin politicians, ministers, officers of the justice department, bankers, film stars, and sports personalities.

At first the Pension Clausewitz was merely a high-class brothel, but the hidden microphones and recording machines of Hitler's Reich were not absent for long. Helmcke discovered that he could add to his profits by combining prostitution with espionage. His first customer was West German counterintelligence, the BfV. They wanted to know who was patronizing his brothel, how frequently they visited him, and any interesting pillow-talk they indulged in. Helmcke supplied this information for a few months and then realized he could double his profits by selling exactly the same sort of intelligence to East Germany. He made contact with the DDR and was soon serving two masters.

In 1962, Helmcke installed a thirty-five-year-old Hungarian refugee named "Josy" Indig as manager of the Pension Clausewitz, allowing him more time to develop his own other interests. In 1963 he started a detective agency which specialized mainly in divorce cases, and opened a news service, the New York Press Agency. This enabled him to carry a press card, of which he was extremely proud. Both these companies were more or less legitimate businesses, employing staff and making a modest profit. A third company he founded in May 1963, a wholesale canned meat business which existed only on paper, was a cover for selling secrets to the East Germans. It was an ideal money-making arrangement. By using the intelligence gathering facilities of his brothel, detective agency, and news service, Helmcke was able to get maximum return on any useful information which came his way. He could sell to either East or West, or use the compromising material to blackmail the victims. Sometimes he did all three at the same time.

Helmcke had discovered a gold mine and the money rolled in. In the next four years he invested his earnings in more night clubs and hotels. He bought a large Mercedes and lived in a luxurious villa. He always tried to appear as a successful and honest businessman. He dressed conservatively in made-to-measure dark blue suits and wore a perfectly adjusted silver gray tie. He had contacts in federal government circles, and was always willing to oblige an influential contact with lavish meals or a beautiful girl. His circle of acquaintances also included gangsters and racketeers. Clients who dialled 32-31-39 to book a girl at the Pension Clausewitz had no idea that among the twenty-four prostitutes Helmcke employed were a number of fully trained swallows supplied by the East German MfS.

Life in the Pension Clausewitz began in late afternoon when the first clients arrived in the central bar. Some would drink with their selected girls before taking them off to one of five comfortably appointed bedrooms which opened off a central corridor. Business was always brisk.

By 1965, the precarious balancing act of the "businessman, journalist, hotel owner, good-food expert, detective, and bar keeper" was almost over. West German counterintelligence was receiving reports of some of the more politically loaded questions which Helmcke's East German-trained girls were asking, and had begun to wonder just how many masters the forty-seven-year-old Berliner was serving. Josy Indig was causing trouble, partly because he felt that Helmcke's latest mistress, a pretty twenty-nine-year-old blonde named Ingeborg Hempel, was having too much say in running the brothel, partly because Helmcke had turned down his suggestion of turning the pension into a house catering to middle-class clients and opening an ultra-expensive and exclusive bordello in Berlin's Grunewald Forest for the top strata of society.

In 1965, Indig tipped off the West Germans that the Clausewitz was being used as a spy center, and it was raided three times. On the first occasion Helmcke's powerful friends managed to help him, but on the third visit the police went straight to the hidden microphones and carried away recording equipment and tapes. The story exploded into the newspapers, with German journalists comparing it to the Profumo scandal in England, speculating on how many high-ranking Germans might be implicated. In fact, when Helmcke was brought before the courts he was sentenced to only a few months' imprisonment, despite the overwhelming evidence of tapes, microphones, and a notebook containing telephone numbers associated with East German intelligence. Later Helmcke was to boast, "Berlin society does not realize what it owes to me. I bought the silence of my girls. If they had talked I would have blown society wide open with scandal." While under arrest he sold the Clausewitz to Ingeborg Hempel for a mere $8,000, but retained his other night clubs and hotels. On his release he went back into business, helped rather than handicapped by the whole affair, which had turned him into a Berlin personality. He was constantly being interviewed and photographed. The Pension Clausewitz saga was even made into a feature film, starring Wolfgang Kieling and Maria Brockerhoff.

The end of the extraordinary Helmcke story was written in 1973 by two men who decided to kidnap Helmcke and ransom him. On Monday, August 13, thirty-year-old Uwe Rohl and twenty-four-year-old Franz Holzer went to Helmcke's Hanseater Club, near Hamburg, and kidnapped another of his mistresses, thirty-nine-year-old Gertie Baetge. She was blindfolded and driven to the apartment of a policeman at Number 4 Mathildestrasse in the St. Pauli area of the city. The policeman was away on vacation in the Black Forest with his family, and the apartment was occupied by thirty-year-old Barbel Rohl, Uwe's wife.

Gertie Baetge was forced to telephone Helmcke in Berlin and ask him to fly to Hamburg to see her on urgent business. Puzzled but anxious, Helmcke drove his dark green Mercedes 250SE to Templehof airport and caught the first available flight. Once in the city he was unable to find the address which Gertie had given him, so he phoned her from a bar. Uwe Rohl drove out and picked him up. It was the last journey the balding Helmcke was to make alive.

As he entered the apartment, Franz Holzer struck him from behind and he was bundled onto the bed. Then Gertie Baetge was driven away from the apartment in a taxi and dropped off in a Hamburg suburb. Back at the apartment Franz Holzer was finding the by-now-conscious Helmcke a more dangerous victim than he had bargained for. Instead of submitting to their ransom demands, the tough ex-paratrooper took great pleasure in describing the excruciating revenge that would attend this impudent piece of folly. Helmcke felt confident he could frighten the amateur gangster into releasing him, but for once he had made a fatal mistake. Instead of talking his way out of trouble, Helmcke signed his own death warrant. Holzer panicked and strangled him with a length of red-and-blue plastic cord, and bundled his corpse into an old trunk. The two men then rented a van and that night drove the truck to the city outskirts to dump it. Anxious that identification should be delayed as long as possible, they first tried to burn Helmcke's body using gas. When the corpse failed to incinerate completely, they heaved the remains back into the truck and dumped them in some bushes near the main highway. Helmcke, who had lived well and dangerously for so long, had his epitaph written by a tough West German policeman. Staring at the mutilated body, he commented, "The only astonishing thing is that it took so long."

In opening the Pension Clausewitz as an espionage brothel, Helmcke was not only restoring the old house to its former role but following a tradition of sexpionage in Germany.

One of the most famous spy brothels in espionage history was the Salon Kitty, set up by Walter Schellenberg in his capacity as head of Department VI, the counterespionage service of the SS in 1935. The Salon Kitty, run by Frau Kitty Schmidt, had a reputation for having the best-stocked bar, the prettiest girls, and the biggest double beds in Berlin. The rooms were wired for sound and Gestapo agents recorded pillow-talk on cumbersome equipment in the basement. According to Schellenberg, the most important victim of a sexpionage entrapment at the Salon Kitty was Count Galeazzo Ciano, the Italian foreign minister. Schellenberg used to patronize the brothel and during his visits, as well as during the regular visits by other top-ranking Nazis, the recording equipment to that particular room was supposed to have been switched off. In fact, the Gestapo kept the machine operating on all occasions, and the recordings were used as ammunition in bitter internal power struggles between leading Nazis.

So successful was this spy brothel that Reinhard Heydrich, the head of Himmler's Security Police, contemplated opening a similar brothel catering to homosexuals. Himmler's personal doctor, Felix Kersten, recalls an encounter with Heydrich in 1941 during which this scheme was discussed. "I had already been told how interested Heydrich was in this house [the female brothel] simply from its value as an intelligence service and also on personal grounds," Kersten remembers. "He had already had successes with its 'ladies.' Beyond that it gave him particular pleasure to have records made of the intimate talks of these important gentlemen, and on suitable occasions, when they crossed his own plans, to make use of such material."

In the early fifties, the East Germans sent an agent into the Federal Republic with orders to train ordinary prostitutes in the arts of sexpionage and to bug hotel bedrooms with cameras and microphones. For legal reasons the man's real name cannot be given and he will be referred to here as Karl Martin.

Martin, a thirty-year-old salesman, was allowed to "escape" from the DDR. Once across the frontier he told West German officials that he wanted to start a new life "free from Communism." After being routinely interrogated, Martin was given permission to settle in the Federal Republic. With funds provided by the MfS he rented a modest villa in the tourist resort of Bad Godesberg, near Bonn. There he worked successfully as a free-lance sales representative until he had established his cover.

Martin's first achievement was to persuade the sixty-year-old landlady of a high-class boarding house popular with foreign diplomats to let him plant microphones in seven bedrooms. These were wired to tape-recorders, which he hid in the attic. For every conversation he taped, the landlady was paid about seventy dollars. The tapes were concealed in food parcels and sent back to East Germany.

Martin briefed his prostitute spies carefully on what questions they should ask their clients, but he left it to their professional skill and experience to devise the best techniques for extracting the necessary secrets. This was a fairly primitive sexpionage operation which yielded only run-of-the-mill information. By using amateur spies Martin was able to build up a network rapidly but it also meant that his security was weak. He had been in operation for only a few months when the CIA broke his cover. Instead of reporting his activities to the German authorities, however, they offered a deal. Martin was considered more valuable out of prison and working as a double agent. He was allowed to send his tapes back to the MfS, but only after they had been heard, duplicated, and approved by the CIA.

Martin was delighted with the arrangement, by which he kept his freedom and received pay from both sides. For the next twelve months the system worked well. Then the Federal authorities discovered his spy ring. Before they could arrest him, the Americans applied pressure on them. They wanted Martin to keep on working as a double agent, because he was providing them with vital information about the way in which DDR espionage operated. During the fifties the German security services were very much under the thumb of the CIA and their security chiefs could do no more than protest at the American interference. Martin was able to operate for another six months before the Germans could finally stand it no longer. In August they worked out plans for Martin's arrest but, when they finally surrounded his house, their man had flown. The CIA, warned that his arrest was imminent, had taken care of him. A court case was the last thing they wanted.

In the mid-sixties, the East Germans started to use a new sexpionage weapon—the blue movie. These were part of a technique to subvert soldiers, NCOs, and junior officers able to provide low-grade but useful military intelligence. The soldiers, from Britain, France, Germany, and America, were invited to parties at which there were secret showings of hard-core pornography. Some information could be obtained merely by careful questioning in the relaxed and comradely atmosphere which followed the film show. East German agents would ply them with drink and, if they thought a man might be particularly useful to them, offer to set him up with a girl friend. A standard sexpionage entrapment could follow, or the girl could merely use her training to glean information from casual conversation. Blue films were found to be such a potent attraction to bored and frustrated soldiers that the East Germans apparently even set up one of their agents with a lavishly equipped secret cinema just to show pornography.

On January 23, 1973, German security agents supported by civilian police moved in on a $20,000 holiday bungalow in the Harz mountains not far from Hanover. With the building surrounded, armed men walked up to the door and sent it crashing open. Fifty-four-year-old Rolf Dreesen, an alleged agent for the DDR, gave up without a struggle. Federal Counterintelligence sources claimed that Dreesen had been sent into Germany on a mission to provide detailed information about British troop movements along the East-West border. It was said that he had been given sufficient funds to buy three hotels in the ski resorts. At one of them, in Andressberg, he had a lavishly equipped cinema constructed in one of the cellars. This, German counterintelligence said, was used for providing free blue-film shows to soldiers. At the time of writing, full details of the Dreesen affair have still not become available.

8

Assault on NATO

In the red safelight glow of a Bonn darkroom, a technician took a thumbnail-wide roll of black-and-white film from the drying cupboard and carried it over to a viewing box. With a magnifying glass, he swiftly examined the oblong negatives, which had been taken by a Minox camera. It was a routine check, carried out at the request of the Bonn police to catch amateur pornographers who sometimes used the inconspicuous miniature cameras. But what the technician now saw through his powerful lens was far from routine. The first nine negatives contained pictures of documents, and on the top of each document was printed the words *"NATO. Security Classification—Cosmic Top Secret."*

The time was 6:20 P.M. The date Friday, September 27, 1968. One of the most astonishing spy dramas in the history of Western security was about to be blown wide open. Within the space of two weeks, a German admiral with nearly forty years' service, who was one of the West's top military planners at Supreme Headquarters Allied Powers Europe, was to be shot dead; the deputy chief of the German secret service would put a bullet through his brain, several other top officials were to die violently, and the alliance was seen to have suffered the most enormous and humiliating security defeat in its history.

When the startled technician hurried out of the darkroom to report his discovery, Frau Trude Helke, the manageress of the photographic shop on Bonn's Sternstrasse, was just locking up for the night. With a few terse words of explanation, he handed her the film and the glass. Frau Helke first checked the negatives and then her pile of order forms to discover the name and address of the customer. It was easily located. The film had been left at the shop the previous Monday and the cost of processing paid in advance. The client had asked that the negatives and a set of prints be posted to him in Belgium. His name was Rear Admiral Hermann Luedke; his address: the officers' quarters, Supreme Headquarters Allied Powers Europe, at Mons. Frau Helke locked the negatives in a drawer and phoned the police. She was put through to Inspector Heinz Rutowski of the Fourteenth (Political) Commissariat, who immediately drove to the shop, where he examined and took charge of the film. Back in his office Rutowski called the Federal Prosecutor's Department for instructions. A porter who answered the phone told him curtly that the office was closed and refused to connect the inspector with anyone. Rutowski's next call was to the headquarters of military counterintelligence. He told them what had been discovered. They did some quick checking and found that Luedke was still in Bonn. He was in fact attending a banquet at military headquarters. At the early age of fifty-seven, he was retiring because of ill-health, and the banquet was a farewell present from his fellow officers. Three senior investigators from the Militärischer Abschirmdienst drove to the building.

In the banqueting hall, Luedke was listening, with suitable modesty, as General Ulrich de Maiziere, the chief of the defense staff, extolled the rear admiral's personal and military virtues. The speeches completed, Luedke posed for photographs beside the general. Afterwards, as he prepared to leave, General de Maiziere drew him to one side. "Can I have a word with you, Hermann?" he asked quietly. "There is a room over there where we can speak in private."

Bewildered, Luedke followed his superior from the banqueting hall, into an office. The door was closed firmly behind him. With an embarrassed air, General de Maiziere nodded towards three civilians. "These gentlemen are from military counterintelligence, Hermann. I am sorry about this. It hardly seems the occasion for such a thing, but the matter is urgent."

Appearing completely mystified, Luedke sat down in a red plush armchair and looked from one security man to the next for enlightenment. The roll of negatives was produced, with a set of hastily made prints. Luedke was asked if he recognized the pictures.

The rear admiral flipped through a group of family snaps and cheerfully admitted he had taken them. Then he came to three photographs of the license plate of his Ford car, frowned thoughtfully, and said that he didn't recall taking those particular shots.

His look of bewilderment changed to one of mild embarrassment when he came to the next batch of prints, which showed an attractive blonde posing partly clothed and completely nude.

It was not until he reached the final nine prints that the rear admiral's expression dramatically altered. Before him lay perfect photocopies of documents relating to NATO's recent headquarters move from France to Belgium. Although a year old, the papers were still classified as top secret. "I never took these pictures," he protested. "I know nothing about the documents. This is some sort of a frame-up. Somebody must have stolen my Minox camera and taken these pictures to incriminate me in espionage. It's monstrous."

The interrogation that followed lasted three hours and left the rear admiral shaken and exhausted. Although the security men were meticulously correct, they were also persistent. Again and again they took Hermann Luedke back over his story and frowned doubtfully at the only explanation for the incriminating photographs he could offer—that they had been planted on him.

It was, on the face of it, an absurd claim. The bulk of the film contained photographs indisputably snaps of his family. He did not deny that others depicted his car's license plate. Under pressure, the embarrassed naval officer even conceded that he had taken the photographs of the nude girl. But the document copying he absolutely denied.

Finally the security men packed away their papers and told Luedke that, for the moment, he was free to go. Why, despite their open suspicions that he had been spying, they released him can only be guessed. Perhaps they were hoping he would panic and incriminate other members of a possible spy ring by making an indiscreet phone call. Maybe they felt that releasing him would do no harm at such an early stage of their investigation.

One German security man suggested to me that their decision sprang from a sense of *Korpsgeist*, the feeling of comradeship between brother officers which exists all over the world, coupled with deference for his high rank. No official explanation has ever been given.

While the confused and indignant rear admiral was being driven to his home outside Bonn, the security men held a conference. On the assumption that Luedke had been spying, the vital questions were: for how long and with what degree of success? His potential as a KGB agent was vast, for Luedke was a man for whom NATO held no secrets. Until the previous January, when he had stepped down on the grounds of ill-health, Luedke had been deputy chief of SHAPE's logistics division, one of the most vital sections of NATO. On this department's efficiency the entire capability of the alliance depends, and Luedke's position at Supreme Headquarters was so elevated that he had been answerable only to the Supreme Commander Allied Powers Europe, Lyman L. Lemnitzer.

NATO has three secrecy grades, which have been adopted by most of the member countries: NATO *Confidential*, NATO *Secret*, and NATO *Cosmic Top Secret*. Any official who is to have access to cosmic secrets must have been given cosmic clearance. This involves a screening process that can last up to two years. Under NATO regulations (Co-ordination of Security Measures in International Command), his personal relations, family background, social life, past career, and education will all be minutely investigated. Luedke had been given cosmic clearance several years before. It would have been impossible for him to do his job without it, for he had one of the most important and responsible jobs in the military alliance. His work included supervising the storage of billions of dollars' worth of military equipment, ranging from Sidewinder air-to-air missiles to F-104 Lockheed Starfighters. He knew the supply routes for distributing munitions, rations, arms, and fuel to NATO forces. He knew top-secret details of the Atlantic convoy system, the location of a network of hidden oil pipelines and ninety-day-reserve dumps throughout Europe, Greece, and Turkey. He knew the sites of nuclear-missile silos from Turkey to the Arctic. He could pinpoint all the atomic minefields that had been sown in key border areas and were designed to be detonated by remote control, to destroy an invading Soviet army. His division supervised and controlled the complex infrastructure of NATO, dealing with such fixed installations as airfields, signals, and telecommunications centers, military headquarters, radar-warning and navigational-aid stations, ports, and missile sites. In short, almost everything that the Russians would like to know about NATO could be found in the brain and in the files of Rear Admiral Luedke.

The next morning, to explain his absence from the house, Luedke put on his olive-green hunting clothes and told his wife he was going shooting. As he often spent his free time in this way, she had no suspicion of the truth. He then drove to military security headquarters, where he was interrogated for six more hours. Once again he protested his innocence and denied any knowledge of the incriminating photographs. When the officers asked him if they could search his house, he readily agreed. On

Sunday, a group of counterintelligence officers drove out to his elegantly furnished home and carried out a detailed search. Perhaps not surprisingly, they found no incriminating documents or spy equipment. Luedke requested, and was granted, permission to travel back to NATO headquarters in Belgium in order to finish clearing personal effects from the officers' quarters in preparation for his retirement. That night he drove to SHAPE, arriving early the following morning.

It was not until his office reopened after the weekend, on Monday, September 30, that Federal Prosecutor Ludwig Martin was informed of the case and decided to leave the matter in the hands of military security. By that time Rear Admiral Luedke had vanished. After clearing out his few belongings from his quarters at SHAPE, he had driven away. The only clue he gave his brother officers was that he intended to do some hunting. Exactly where he went or what happened to him after he left Mons remains a complete mystery. He was not, apparently, in the hands of military counterintelligence, nor did he attempt to leave the country. It is possible he hid out under a false name while trying to contact his KGB controller for orders and help. What is certain is that eight days later he was shot dead.

Luedke's death was to trigger a macabre wave of suicides, arrests, and a spy hysteria that shook NATO and the Federal Republic to their foundations. As disaster piled upon disaster, CIA, SIS, and SDECE agents in the Republic were ordered to make their own assessments of the damage. Soon, over scrambled embassy phones and via enciphered teleprinter messages, they were telling their superiors the results of their investigations. What they, and NATO security officers, discovered has never been made public. A shroud of secrecy descended on the whole affair from the moment the rear admiral's body was discovered.

Was Luedke a spy or had he been framed? Did he kill himself, as the authorities asserted, or was he murdered to silence him?

My own investigations have suggested the following scenario for the events that led up to, and followed, that dramatic moment in the Bonn darkroom when the secret documents were spotted. Although Luedke strenuously protested his innocence during the two periods of interrogation, my information says that he was an important if reluctant KGB spy. Although he operated to full effect for only a matter of weeks, in that short time he was able to pass to the Soviets a vast range of detailed information about NATO. At the same time, his bewildered indignation over the nine compromising negatives was perfectly genuine. He had *not* taken photographs of the classified documents. He *had* been framed. The men who did it were his spy masters, the KGB.

Why should they sell out their own man? What prompted them to turn over a valuable agent to Federal Counterintelligence?

The answers to these questions provide a fascinating insight into the treacherous and complex world of international espionage.

On August 20, 1968, when Warsaw Pact tanks and troops poured across the Czech frontier to bring down the liberal government of Alexander Dubcek, hundreds of Czechs fled to the West. Among these refugees were a number of disillusioned secret service officers who were only too pleased to sell what information they possessed to the CIA, the SIS, or any intelligence service that offered the right sort of incentives. One such man was General Jan Senj, who arrived in Bonn in late August and immediately made himself known to his opposite numbers in the Federal Intelligence Service, the BND. As party secretary assigned to the Czech Ministry of Defense, Senj had regularly attended Warsaw Pact meetings and knew a great deal about KGB spy networks operating inside NATO. Acting on his information, the Federal security services were able to close the net around a number of KGB spies, one of the most important being Nihat Imre, a high-ranking Turkish official in the NATO finance department, whose story will be told later. Faced with this disaster, the KGB case officer in charge of the espionage assault on NATO set about devising a plan that would enable him to salvage what he could from his crumbling networks. Since several of these were clearly going to be closed down anyhow, the decision was taken to gain as much propaganda as possible out of the affair. If NATO could be shown to be riddled with traitors and KGB agents, it might have a disastrous effect on public confidence in the alliance and, more important, prove seriously detrimental to relations among the member countries. It was known in Moscow that the United States, as the country with the most military secrets to lose, was far from happy about the security risks posed by sharing such knowledge with other NATO countries, especially West Germany.

The plan that was evolved required the sacrifice of Hermann Luedke, but this was hardly a significant loss. It was likely that the rear admiral would, in any event, be detected quite soon as a result of Jan Senj's disclosures, and even if he did slip through the security net, his early retirement would soon make him useless to the KGB. By framing him in such a way that the treason of a high-ranking NATO officer must become public knowledge, they hoped to inflict maximum political damage on the organization.

They probably had few qualms about disposing of their agent in this brutal fashion because the rear admiral had never been more than a reluctant spy. He was a man forced against his will to turn traitor, for whom the knowledge of his treason was a terrible burden.

Luedke had been recruited into the KGB in 1966 via a sexpionage entrapment carried out in Paris. A married man, with five children, the rear admiral's exuberant personality and youthful looks had gained him the nickname "Sonny Boy." He was popular amongst his fellow officers and attractive to women; an attraction he was happy to exploit, both to entice them into his bed and to persuade them to pose for his camera. An enthusiastic amateur photographer, Luedke took his photographs with a secondhand Minox he had bought cheaply in 1962; his favorite subjects were pretty girls posing in the nude.

He had been in the KGB files as a potential spy for many years when, in the spring of 1966, the trap was finally sprung. In a Left Bank night club, Luedke was maneuvered into a meeting with a beautiful twenty-three-year-old French girl who was a KGB swallow. The same evening, they went back to the woman's flat in the Rue St. Honoré, where he took photographs of her in the nude before they made love. After that first meeting they saw one another regularly over a period of some weeks, and the rear admiral soon built up an intimate portfolio of the girl in suggestive nude poses. Finally the trap was sprung, and the horrified officer was confronted with a set of pictures he had not taken—a dozen glossy photographs of his love-making. The price asked for these pictures, which could wreck his marriage and harm his career if made public, was intentionally modest. All that was demanded in exchange for the negatives were some classified documents of trivial importance. Luedke took what seemed the easiest way out, and supplied the material for copying. The whole transaction was photographed. Luedke was handed the negatives of his love affair as promised, but was then told that photographs of him handing over NATO secret papers would be on the desk of the Supreme Commander within the hour unless he cooperated. Luedke miserably agreed to spy.

At first the Russians made only minor demands on their new agent, merely requesting sufficient secret information to leave Luedke in no doubt that they meant business. Their reason for keeping the rear admiral on ice was simple. Once they made full use of him, the surge of high-level military intelligence reaching Moscow was bound to be detected by Western security, as Soviet military tactics, troop dispositions, and contingency plans were adapted to fit in with the fresh information. After a while, suspicion was bound to fall on Luedke. Traps would be set and the rear admiral detected. His life as a spy, given all the luck in the world, was not likely to be a long one. The KGB waited until the time arrived when they could make the best possible use of their uniquely placed agent. That moment came in April 1967, following the transfer of SHAPE headquarters, with the rest of NATO's command structure, from France to Belgium. The pressure on Luedke abruptly increased. As well as photographing top-secret documents, he was ordered to subvert suitable members of his staff and other NATO employees, either by bribery or through blackmail. Luedke had no choice but to obey. His health deteriorated rapidly under the strain. The high-living Luedke of the Paris days vanished, never to return. From being a cheerful extrovert, he became irritable and withdrawn. Although he still enjoyed photographing pretty girls in the nude, he spent most of his free time watching television or reading in the bachelor officers' quarters. On his free weekends he would either drive to Bonn to see his wife and children or go hunting in the Eifel forests. On some of these trips he would meet his KGB controller to hand over rolls of microfilm, shot on his Minox, or receive orders.

On September 1, 1967, his importance to the Russians increased because of structural changes inside NATO. The production logistics and infrastructure division in which Luedke was employed became the defense support division, widening its activities to include weapons research. In the words of an unclassified NATO document: "Its main role in the armaments and logistics field remains to promote the most efficient use of the resources of the alliance for the equipment and support of its forces."

Luedke was forced to photograph an increasing number of documents. His health went downhill fast. In January 1968, doctors advised early retirement, and Luedke thankfully used this as a way out of the nightmare. He announced that he would leave the service at the end of September. In those final few months, the KGB's determination to extract the last scrap of value from their victim led to almost impossible demands on Luedke. On one occasion he was ordered not to photograph, but to steal parts of the guidance system of a Hawk missile.

Though Luedke had angrily protested that it was an impossible assignment, he finally managed to obtain the required equipment.

The Hawk, its name taken from "Homing All the Way Killer," is a solid-propellant surface-to-air missile for use against low-flying aircraft and ballistic missiles. It is equipped with a high-explosive blast fragmentation warhead and homing radar. At that time the homing device was still top secret, and it was this the Russians wanted to examine. Luedke transported it to his meeting place in the Eifel hills, where it was studied and photographed by his KGB controller and a Soviet electronics expert. The men then ordered Luedke to replace it, but he refused point blank, saying it would be far too dangerous. Eventually they agreed to get rid of it for him, and did so in the most casual manner possible, dumping the top-secret equipment on a rubbish heap outside the village of Dernau, where it was later recovered by NATO security men.

The plan to deliver Hermann Luedke to Federal Intelligence involved the KGB in no real difficulties. An agent working at SHAPE obtained some year-old documents which were still classified as Cosmic Top Secret. These were photographed by a Minox camera. The agent then took a number of close-up pictures of Luedke's Ford in the SHAPE parking lot. This was done to link the film positively to the rear admiral. Then followed the only really risky part of the entire operation. A KGB technical expert broke into Luedke's apartment in the officers' quarters and switched their film for the one already in his camera. Luedke never noticed the substitution and used up the roll taking nude studies and some family snaps during his next visit to Bonn. He dropped the finished film at the photographic store on the Sternstrasse for processing and printing. Even if the technician had failed to spot the documents on the negatives, they were bound to be seen when enlargements were made. The KGB knew that the shop would immediately contact the police. By framing Luedke in this way, they had made it virtually certain that news of the astonishing discovery would leak to the press.

Shattered by the inexplicable pictures, Luedke seems to have gone to ground. During the next week he must have tried desperately to contact his controller to get assistance. But the KGB man refused to see him.

On October 8, however, Hermann Luedke did get the long-awaited invitation to a meeting on the Immerath hunting preserve in the Eifel hills. He dressed in his olive-green shooting clothes and flung his Mauser rifle onto the back seat of his car before driving to the meeting, and his death!

At around three o'clock that afternoon a shot was heard by nearby villagers. Ninety minutes later, a farmer, Alois Zenzen, found Luedke's body slumped beside his car on the outskirts of a wood. He had been killed with his own sporting rifle by a soft-nosed bullet which had entered his body at the base of the spine and traveled diagonally upwards before hitting the chest. A doctor who was called to the scene ruled out any possibility of suicide, and the local police agreed. However, the post-mortem finding was that Luedke had killed himself or shot himself accidentally. A police spokesman told the press, "It appears he flung his hunting rifle into the back of the car without fixing the safety catch. When he climbed into the car the rifle must have gone off, shooting him in the back." In tests, carried out during the research for this book, using a similar type of rifle and Ford, it proved impossible to duplicate the kind of accident situation which, it is claimed, cost the rear admiral his life. Even if the Mauser had discharged accidentally, the bullet could not have entered Luedke's body in the way it did. In fact, it is unlikely that he would have been hit at all. Bearing in mind that Luedke was an experienced hunter and an expert on firearms, who was hardly likely to treat his rifle in the casual, amateurish way suggested by the authorities, the accident theory seems totally discredited. The idea that he would commit suicide in this highly involved and difficult manner is equally improbable.

We are left with murder—the deliberate slaying of the officer in order to silence him. If this is indeed what happened, then Luedke must have known and trusted his killer to allow him to get into the back of the car beside his loaded rifle.

The obvious suspect is the KGB, who, having set up Luedke's betrayal, decided to silence him before he could give too much away to Federal Counterintelligence. At first the rumor was that he had been "terminated" by a professional hit-man from 2 Dzerzhinsky Square. But if the Russians had decided to silence Luedke, why had they waited so long before doing so? In fact, it was very much in the interest of the KGB that Luedke should be arrested and put on trial, so that all the horrifying security weaknesses of the alliance could be brought into the glare of international publicity.

A more likely explanation for the shooting, and one supported by information I received in Paris, is that a Western security service, possibly the CIA or the BND, decided to silence Luedke and so avert the need for an embarrassing trial.

Luedke's shooting was one of the earliest in a series of inexplicable deaths that occurred during the next two weeks, but it was not the first. Some three hours before the rear admiral was killed, another high-ranking German officer died of gunshot wounds. This time it really was suicide. The victim was fifty-six-year-old Major General Horst Wendland, deputy head of the BND. A dedicated and long-serving counterintelligence officer, Wendland had been under political and professional pressure for some time. In April 1968, the founder and head of the BND, sixty-six-year-old Reinhard Gehlen, a former Wehrmacht intelligence officer, had finally retired. One of two candidates for taking over the leadership, Wendland, had been regarded by many as Gehlen's natural successor, and he was supported by the majority of the BND staff. His rival, Lieutenant General Gerhard Wessel, had the support of Gehlen himself. In October 1968, the decision was made that Wessel, whose easy, extrovert character contrasted favorably with Wendland's remote and bureaucratic personality, should get the job. It was a bitter disappointment to Wendland, who was, moreover, in poor physical health after years of dedicated service to the BND.

The discovery of Luedke's treachery and the knowledge that General Jan Senj's disclosures had revealed major KGB infiltration of NATO were the final blows. At nine o'clock on October 8, he kissed his wife, Ilse, good-by and drove from his house in Feldafing to Pullach Camp, headquarters of the BND. He attended a conference, read and corrected some documents, and then told his secretary that he was not to be disturbed for the next few minutes. At about 11:50 A.M., he took a 9mm Browning hi-power from his desk drawer and shot himself in the right temple. His body was discovered, by his secretary, at 12:07 P.M.

These two deaths, one suicide, the other almost certainly murder, were sensational enough. But they were followed in rapid succession by ten other deaths. Some were suicides unconnected with espionage, which would have passed almost unreported under normal circumstances; others involved agents recruited by Luedke who killed themselves rather than face arrest and disgrace. It is often hard to distinguish between the two because of the tight security screen thrown around the whole affair, but the following seem to be the most likely contenders for the espionage-suicide combination.

Frau Edeltraud Grapentin, fifty-two, a divorced filing clerk who had worked in the Federal Press and Information Office since 1952. She died from an overdose of sleeping tablets on October 14. Personal problems were the official explanation for her death.

Lieutenant Colonel Johannes Grimm, fifty-four, a staff officer in the logistics and war mobilization department of the German Ministry of Defense, shot himself at his desk on October 18 and died three hours later in the hospital. An official spokesman claimed that the man took his life because he believed he had cancer. Friends say that this is nonsense, that he had been told some hours before his death that he did not have any incurable disease.

On October 21, the police announced the death of Dr. Hans Heinrich Schenk, forty, a senior official in the economics department, who had hanged himself in a closet at his Cologne apartment a week earlier. All reports of his death had been kept secret until this announcement.

Three days later the body of Gerhard Boehm, sixty-one, an employee of the Defense Ministry, was dragged out of the Rhine. His briefcase, hat, coat, and a suicide note to his family ("I am sorry to go this way") were found by a Bonn bridge on October 21 following an anonymous tip-off. The police claimed he had killed himself because he was depressed after being passed over for promotion. Immediately after Boehm's disappearance, however, a leak from the security services had said that it was feared he had fled to East Germany.

No fewer than six high-ranking East German agents, all of them scientists and physicists who had come to West Germany some years earlier, as refugees from Communism, took advantage of the confusion to return home. One who did not make it was Dr. Harald Gottfried, thirty-three, a physicist at the Karlsruhe Atomic Center. He was arrested and is said to have confessed to passing atomic secrets to the East Germans. The prosecution claimed that more than 800 photographs of classified documents had been found at his home. While all this was going on, SHAPE headquarters was the scene of frantic activity as officials tried desperately to minimize the damage to Western defenses. Some 16,000 tactical nuclear warheads were resited, supply dumps were moved, ciphers and codes changed, and the "Strike Plan"—NATO's over-all contingency strategy against a Warsaw Pact attack on the West—reviewed.

From all points of view, the KGB spy ring inside NATO had been staggeringly successful, causing short-term security damage and incalculable long-term harm to the delicately balanced relationships among the member nations. But perhaps the success of the operation becomes less surprising when it is discovered that behind the whole affair was one of the most skilled and experienced masters of subversion in the history of espionage, the former British double agent Kim Philby.

Philby was born in India on New Year's Day, 1912, the son of a British government official. Although christened Harold Adrian Russell Philby, the boy soon came to be known as Kim, after Rudyard Kipling's fictional hero. In 1924, his parents returned to England, where Kim won a scholarship to Westminster, his father's old school. From the start, he was a boy of exceptional promise, fluent in several languages, intelligent, hard-working, tidy, and obedient.

Westminster is one of Britain's oldest schools. Standing in the shadow of the Houses of Parliament, it is very much a part of the Establishment; its students play a part in the ritual of a coronation, and six seats are permanently reserved for them in the public gallery of the House of Commons. As a boarder, Philby slept in one of forty tiny bedroom cubicles and ate his meals in the fourteenth-century dining hall. At Westminster, Philby underwent two experiences of some significance to his future development. His father, a religious skeptic, had brought his son up in a tradition of agnosticism. Westminster, like most British public schools, was strongly religious, and Philby, an obedient child, felt his loyalty torn between father and school. Eventually it led to a nervous breakdown. As in many single-sex boarding schools, homosexuality was rife at Westminster, and Philby indulged in it with the other boys. Later he talked openly of having "buggered and been buggered" at school. The result of these experiences, coupled, perhaps, with the fact that his formative years were spent abroad, was to make him an outsider—within the British Establishment but not a part of it; a man who felt no loyalty towards his country and what it stood for. From Westminster he went to Trinity College, Cambridge, to read history. There his political awakening took place. Amongst the students in his year were a number of ex-miners who had made the daunting journey from pit face to scholarship by means of funds provided by a workers' educational association. From these men Philby absorbed grass-roots socialism. He became a political activist, with leanings farther and farther to the left. Eventually he joined the Communist party of Great Britain, which had been founded in 1920, although he never held a party card. This fact was to prove important when, probably in 1934, he was recruited by Soviet intelligence. It means that, although a dedicated Communist, he was, so far as the British authorities were concerned, politically clean.

When the Spanish Civil War broke out, Philby went to Spain as a free-lance journalist and a Soviet agent. His cover was precarious and almost collapsed within a few weeks of his arrival when he was hauled in for interrogation by the civilian police. He escaped arrest, and almost certain execution, only by eating his code book. Soon after World War II started, Philby was recruited into the SIS by Guy Burgess, a homosexual, a Soviet agent, and a trusted member of British intelligence. In this way began Philby's extraordinary double life as a British agent and Soviet spy. With his quick mind, dedication, and attractive personality, Philby rose swiftly through the ranks of the Secret Intelligence Service. In the early years of the war there was little conflict of interest between his work for the British and his spying for the Russians. Since both countries were fighting Nazi Germany, the Russians had easy access to all the secrets they needed. It was not until 1945 and the start of the Cold War that Philby the KGB agent really came into his own. Then one of his important functions was to warn the Soviet's about counterintelligence operations planned against their networks. One example will demonstrate how effective he was in this role.

Soon after the war, a top KGB agent in Istanbul, Konstantin Volkoff, who was operating as a "legal" attached to the Soviet Consulate General, contacted the British with a request for political asylum. In exchange for a new life in the West, plus more than $100,000, he was prepared to give the British a list of all Soviet agents in the area and, far more important, the names of three high-ranking Soviet agents operating inside the British intelligence organizations. The British consul general sent a top-secret cable to London asking for instructions. The case was passed to the SIS for attention, and the file dropped onto the desk of Kim Philby. A few days later a Soviet military aircraft landed at Istanbul airport. Before astonished Turkish officials could make any move to approach the plane, a Russian car screeched across the runway right up to the aircraft, whose cargo hatch had been swung down as soon as it stopped moving. A stretcher carrying a heavily bandaged figure was dragged from the car and manhandled aboard the aircraft. Moments later, the plane lifted from the runway, taking the unfortunate Volkoff back to a grim fate in Moscow. Philby was able to remain an active double agent until 1963, when he thought it wiser to defect to Russia.

In Moscow he was hailed as a hero, and provided with a large Moscow flat in addition to a second home in the country. When he first arrived in the Soviet Union, Philby's health was poor, aggravated by the tensions of his last months in the West and by a drinking problem. The Russians restored him to health, dried him out, and put him to work as a consultant in a comfortable office at KGB headquarters. His chief target was NATO.

The North Atlantic Treaty Organization had been born on April 4, 1949, when twelve Western countries signed a mutual-defense pact. In 1955, the Federal Republic of Germany had become a member. Although an essential addition to NATO from a strategic point of view, her membership produced security weaknesses which the Russians were quick to exploit. Ever since the end of the war, West Germany has had the unhappy distinction of being one of the most spied-upon countries in the world. A report published in 1966 by the Rome Ministry of Defense, entitled *Internal Security*, estimated that by the end of 1959 there were 6,000 full-time Eastern-bloc agents operating from secure cover in the Republic, backed up by 10,000 "visiting" agents. Six years later the figures appear to have stabilized at around 8,000 full-time agents and 12,000 migratory spies sent over on specific missions. "We have got spies like other people have got mice," admitted one German official grimly.

The assault on NATO directed by Kim Philby involved techniques of both classical and electronic espionage. Professional agents, planted in lowly positions in the alliance, were to be allowed to grow into positions of power before starting work for Moscow. Amateur spies, like Luedke, were recruited through bribery or blackmail, including sexpionage entrapments.

When Philby was brought in to assist with the assault on NATO, the KGB already had several active networks inside the organization. One of them, operating from Italy, was led by Angela Maria Rinaldi and her husband, Giorgio. Both were enthusiastic parachutists, and while giving skydiving displays used the opportunity to fly over NATO bases and to photograph secret areas and missile locations. By 1963, Italian counterintelligence, supported by the CIA, was on the trail of the "Red Tsarina" and her husband, although her network continued to supply useful medium-grade information to Moscow right up to their arrest in 1967. Despite the attraction of operating through West Germany, Philby's first thrust was made from the south, via Turkey. In 1964, he sent out orders to KGB agents in Ankara to discover a suitably placed national who could be persuaded to spy for them. Within a matter of months they had done so.

The man's name was Nihat Imre and he was a high-ranking official in NATO's finance department. Imre was either bribed into espionage or persuaded to spy for Russia on ideological grounds, but his activities were kept at a low key until 1965, when he was appointed an A7 official, the highest administrative rank in NATO, as chief financial controller. Imre had access to all top-secret documents, because no project could receive financing unless the documents had his signature.

Imre proved a valuable agent, and the KGB rewarded Philby for his success by giving him one of the highest Soviet decorations, the Red Banner of Labor.

With Imre working efficiently for them, Philby turned his attention to Germany. Luedke was recruited, along with a number of other agents, and a vast range of secrets began to flow back to Dzerzhinsky Square. The mid-sixties was a time of confusion for NATO and of opportunity for the Soviet Union. In March 1966, President de Gaulle announced that France intended to withdraw from the alliance and ordered his former allies to remove from French territory the international headquarters outside Paris, as well as all military bases and installations not coming under direct French control. As a result, NATO was thrown into confusion, and security, always weak, became even more vulnerable. New headquarters for SHAPE were established near Mons, in Belgium, where a vast modern complex was rushed up on flat, marshy countryside. Other buildings in and around Brussels, forty miles from Mons, were taken over to house NATO's massive bureaucracy. In the autumn of 1966, the first of hundreds of heavily guarded military convoys set off from Paris carrying secret documents and files. On March 30, 1967, the flags of the fourteen member nations were lowered for the last time at Rocquencourt, outside Paris, to be raised the following morning at Mons. On the surface the changeover had been a smooth, precise operation. In reality it had been a period of hectic muddle, in which the KGB spies flourished.

The information provided by General Jan Senj was the first major blow to Philby's smoothly functioning networks. Imre was identified and then filmed by a hidden television camera as he photographed secret documents in his Brussels office. He was allowed to return to Ankara, where he was arrested and tried by a military court.

ASSAULT ON NATO

But before the collapse occurred, the KGB was able to pull off at least one other coup against NATO. Although it may not have been the most serious from a security point of view, it was certainly the most dramatic. In an operation that combined nerveless impudence with high comedy, three Soviet agents managed to steal a complete guided missile and then drive it halfway across Germany disguised as a roll of carpet.

The operation was carried out by a three-man team led by a German architect, Manfred Ramminger, a thirty-year-old playboy spy with a Walter Mitty complex. A man of private means, Ramminger's favorite hobby, until he met a Pole named Josef Linowsky, was racing Ferraris at the Nuremberg track. Then he was introduced to another way of living dangerously—espionage as an employee of the KGB.

Josef Linowsky had been born near Warsaw and trained as a master locksmith. In 1941, he was rounded up by the Nazis and sent to Auschwitz concentration camp. By a miracle he survived, emerging from the experience with such a deep loathing of Germans and Germany that when his twenty-seven-year-old Polish wife, Helena, asked for a divorce, he refused, telling her, "I will never take the risk that you might marry a German, so that our son will have to call some German swine daddy."

In 1951, he applied to the Polish Military Mission in Berlin for permission to visit relatives in Warsaw. This was granted. While in Warsaw he was recruited into the Polish intelligence service, and then allowed to return to West Germany. He was never more than a low-grade agent, sending in what snippets of information he could glean in return for a few hundred marks a year. After his arrest, Helena recalled that, although often penniless, Josef always seemed to get hold of money when he really needed it. He also received a great deal of mail from abroad. "Once I had opened some of his letters out of curiosity—when he found out he beat me up," she said.

In 1958, Linowsky met Manfred Ramminger and was impressed by his life style and obvious wealth. Ramminger had just divorced his wife and was living alone in a large house at Ingolstadt, in Bavaria. Linowsky, who had left his wife and son, was looking for somewhere to live. He and Ramminger became friendly, and the architect offered to let him move into his home. There is no suggestion that a homosexual relationship developed; it was far more a master-and-servant relationship, with Ramminger glad to have somebody to handle the more tedious chores of managing a household, and Linowsky pleased to share the architect's fast-moving life style. In order to earn a few marks for his trouble, Linowsky filed a routine report with Polish intelligence about his new friend.

At his trial Ramminger claimed that he was recruited into the KGB in 1967 when he visited Moscow in order to negotiate a contract for the design of an animal-fodder factory. During his visit, he claimed, he was told by the KGB that the contract, worth some $50,000, would be his provided he became a Soviet agent. Other evidence suggests that Ramminger was recruited into the KGB as early as 1963 and received training in Moscow.

In February 1967, Ramminger made a vital contract. While playing cards in an Ingolstadt club, he met Wolf Diethard Knoppe, a thirty-three-year-old pilot attached to the 74th Starfighter squadron at the nearby Zell air base. At the time, the Starfighter, with a high record of crashes, was regarded as an unreliable and dangerous aircraft to fly. A popular German joke of the period asked, "How do you get hold of a Starfighter?" to which the answer was, "Buy half an acre of land and wait a week." Despite the hazards of his profession, Hauptfeldwebel Knoppe still found life too tame. During his off-duty periods he liked to drive fast cars (he owned a twelve-cylinder Maserati) and ride spirited horses. Like Ramminger, he was constantly looking for ways to make his life more interesting and exciting. The men soon became firm friends. When Knoppe complained that he had failed to be elected secretary of his local riding club, Ramminger set up a rival club and made him president. During their meetings Knoppe would often joke about the lack of security at the Zell air force base. "You could walk in and steal a Starfighter any night of the week," he told Ramminger. This interesting information was sent straight back to Moscow.

In addition to fast cars and horses, Knoppe's main interest was women, especially long-legged, fair-haired girls. Ramminger, ordered by Moscow to encourage his friend in this pursuit, was given funds to rent Knoppe three luxurious apartments in Neuberg, which the pilot later described to friends as "my love nests." This was a sexpionage ploy with a difference. Knoppe needed no help in finding and seducing pretty girls, nor was there any need for blackmail entrapment. The pilot was only too willing to co-operate with Ramminger and Linowsky in any scheme that offered excitement and helped him maintain his lavish standard of living.

By the spring of 1967, the time had come to put Knoppe to his first test. A great deal of effort and money had been spent on him, and Ramminger wanted to show results.

Knoppe obtained a set of passes that enabled Linowsky to get inside the Zell base. Using his lock-picking skills, the Pole entered a top-security warehouse and managed to steal a Litton LM III navigation box, claimed to be the most sophisticated instrument of its kind in the West. This equipment was smuggled to Moscow in a consignment of miniskirts. The next coup was to steal an inertial navigation platform worth more than $100,000 from the Hanover industrial fair. Once again Knoppe's contacts and Linowsky's skill with locks proved a perfect partnership.

After this the KGB was confident that the group could achieve an even greater triumph—the theft of a complete Phantom. Eighty-eight of these aircraft had been ordered by the Luftwaffe and were due to arrive within a few months. Moscow told Ramminger to lie low and wait his chance. Then Knoppe suggested an alternative weapon, which could be stolen with little difficulty and, he believed, without prejudicing the aircraft theft. Ramminger agreed and decided, on his own initiative, to steal a Sidewinder AIM 9E air-to-air guided missile.

The Sidewinder, named after a species of rattlesnake, had first entered service in 1956, and by the time US production ceased in 1962, more than 60,000 of the solid-fuel missiles had been made. Production was continued throughout the sixties by a European consortium.

After news of the theft had become public, Western intelligence leaked a series of stories to the world's press claiming that it was a stupid robbery of no value to the Russians, since the mass-produced missile could be bought almost across the counter from any arms dealer. What this disinformation story did not add was that the AIM 9E was fitted with a sophisticated secret homing device that greatly improved its low-altitude performance. It was this system, rather than the bulky rocket itself, that was of value to the Soviet Union. Ramminger, lacking the necessary expertise to remove the homing system, decided to take the complete nine-foot-long, 160-pound rocket. Knoppe carried out a careful reconnaissance of the storage sheds and supplied Linowsky with details of the locks. After studying the air station security schedules, the pilot suggested October 7 as the most suitable date. The base was infested with rats, and the commander had given orders for vermin exterminators to put down poisoned meat during that night. Because of this, the civilian dog handlers had been ordered to keep their animals caged. It was a stroke of fortune that removed the last serious obstacle to success.

Knoppe gave Linowsky a pass to enter the base and, after he had done so, hid him until nightfall. A few hours before the theft, the pilot walked to a selected spot at the perimeter fence and cut out a large section of the steel mesh, fixing it in place loosely so that it would pass a casual examination. Soon after midnight he fetched the Pole from his hiding place, and they made their way to the missile storage place. Linowsky got inside without difficulty. With equal ease he released a Sidewinder missile from its locked mounts and helped Knoppe place it on a two-wheeled barrow. The tires squeaking loudly, the men then retraced their steps, closing and relocking the doors behind them.

The missile was lifted out through the perimeter fence and into a nearby lane, where Ramminger was waiting beside Knoppe's Maserati. The missile was so long that they had to break the rear window to get it into the car at all. To cover up the protruding snout, Knoppe took a length of old carpet from the trunk and wound it around the six-inch-diameter missile. They then drove over 200 miles across Germany to an apartment in Krefeld that Ramminger had rented for the operation. There they unpacked the missile from the car and managed to split it into two parts, which were crated up and labeled "business samples." While Knoppe made the long trip back to Zell, Ramminger drove with the crates to Düsseldorf airport and freighted them via Copenhagen to Moscow. The cargo manifests identified the contents as "samples."

With his crates safely loaded aboard the aircraft, Manfred Ramminger bought a ticket on the same flight. When he landed in Moscow some hours later, however, a shock awaited him. The crates and Sidewinder had vanished. Without leaving the airport terminal, Ramminger flew back to Europe to find out what had gone wrong. In Düsseldorf he discovered that the crates had been returned from Copenhagen because of an error in the documents that accompanied them. He was politely asked to fill in the missing details. Coolly, Ramminger did so, and the crates went to Moscow without further trouble. For their efforts Ramminger and his associates received nearly $34,000.

Ramminger's network was destroyed by its own lack of security. An air force sergeant, sent by his wife to pick parsley in their back garden, wandered along the boundary fence and discovered the gaping hole in the wire. A quick investigation revealed the theft of the missile, and the trail led straight to Knoppe and, through him, to Linowsky and Ramminger. They were arrested, tried, and found guilty of espionage. Linowsky was sentenced to four years; Knoppe was given a three-year term. Ramminger, as the leader and a suspected professional KGB agent, was jailed for seven years. But he served only part of that sentence. If the Russians were annoyed that, by stealing the Sidewinder without orders he had probably cost them a Phantom, they clearly did not harbor a grudge. In August 1971, during one of the biggest spy swaps, some twenty East German agents were exchanged for six West Germans serving long sentences for political offenses. High on the list of those exchanged was the dashing architect Manfred Ramminger.

9

On Her Majesty's Sexual Service

In July 1970, small advertisements for a health club offering "relief massage" started to appear in Belfast newspapers. In the same months, residents in the city's Antrim and Malone Roads started to notice an unusual amount of activity around two houses in the neighborhood. At all hours of the night cars would pull up, men would hurry from them into the houses and then depart an hour or so later. It soon became clear to the indignant residents that well-patronized brothels were operating in their midst. What the outraged Belfast citizens had no way of knowing was that the two houses and the "health club" on Malone Road were owned and managed by the British government. They were part of a sexpionage operation organized by the Security Service with the cooperation of Scotland Yard.

The order to set up these spy brothels came after an intelligence failure by the Special Branch of the Royal Ulster Constabulary, a traditional source of British Army information. By completely underestimating the strength of Catholic feeling and the extent to which the Irish Republican Army was organized in Belfast, the British had brought to an end the brief "honeymoon" period between their troops and the Catholic population of the city. On June 27, during a siege by Protestants of a church in East Belfast, Provisional gunmen had come into organized action for for the first time. Following the army's curfew and house searches of the Falls Road area, a Catholic stronghold, rioting broke out. By the end of the week of July 3, ten people had been killed, 276 injured, and damage to property, assessed at more than a million dollars, had been caused. Surveying the destruction gloomily, a British diplomat remarked to a friend: "That was the greatest miscalculation I have ever seen made in the course of my whole life." It was a miscalculation based on faulty intelligence and one that was to have both political and security repercussions. The Ulster Cabinet pushed through legislation that would enable the authorities to arrest *anybody* present at a riot no matter how innocent their involvement, and the Security Servicemen met officers from Army Intelligence and the Special Branch to devise new ways of gaining reliable information. One of the techniques approved was the setting up of brothels.

To set up and control the brothels the Security Service formed a special intelligence unit with offices in Churchill House, a government building in Belfast. The unit was staffed by a number of officers who had seen active service in the Middle East and subsequently became known to members of the IRA as the Aden Gang. Their top-floor office was given an innocent-sounding cover and fitted out with alarms, hidden TV cameras, which could observe all visitors to the floor, and bulletproof doors. The officers involved went armed at all times.

In order to run the brothels along professional lines, the unit called on the services of Britain's uncrowned king of vice, a Londoner who earned more than $6 million from prostitution during his long career in Soho. This man lived in great luxury and owned a Georgian mansion in one of the most fashionable parts of the city. His neighbours believed him a wealthy banker or company director. He tipped waiters $25, and never carried less than $1,200 in cash. He claimed that he changed his Rolls-Royce as often as his girl friend changed her hair style and boasted that he bribed Scotland Yard detectives to ensure that he and his syndicate were left in peace. One senior officer is said to have received $3,000 a week over a long period.

In 1970, believing that co-operation would make life easier for him in Britain, this man agreed to help establish the brothels. He flew to Belfast, where he was met by a senior detective who was acting as a liaison officer between the Security Service and the Royal Ulster Constabulary. A Ministry of Defense car took them to the heavily guarded Security Service headquarters at Thipveal Barracks, near Lisburn, where the operation was outlined to him. He remained ten days in the city, helping to select suitable premises and advising on management techniques. During his stay in Ulster he was provided with an armed bodyguard.

On his return to London, the man started recruiting prostitutes to staff the brothels. The girls were selected for their brains as much as their good looks and warned that they would be taking part in a risky but rewarding enterprise. The impression most of them got was that they would be entertaining British officers in army brothels. In return for a short term of duty in Ulster they were to be paid $1,000 a week, the money going directly into a UK bank. They were told to sign the Official Secrets Act and warned that, having done so, they could be jailed if they talked about their experiences. The man was paid only expenses for his part in the operation, but, as usual, he received a large part of the money paid over to his girls.

The main objective of this sexpionage operation was to compromise important Ulster men in order to blackmail them, either for information or into becoming informers. To do this, hidden cameras were fitted in the walls and ceilings of the bedrooms.

The prices charged by the establishments were high, but not outrageous. In the "health studio" a man paid between $12, for a "basic" massage, and $40, for a "full-body" massage. In the Antrim Road brothel the charge of $100 for straight intercourse was designed to attract a wealthier and more exclusive type client. At all the houses girls were young, pretty, and willing.

The decor of the health studio was fairly spartan. It had a small, poorly equipped gymnasium, sauna bath, and solarium, but the majority of the clients ignored these keep-fit facilities. By walking across the reception area and through a rear door, they found themselves in a dimly lit corridor flanked by a series of curtained cubicles. These were furnished with an iron-framed bed, a wooden chair, and a wardrobe. The walls were covered with large mirrors, which enabled the customer to see everything that was happening and allowed photographs to be taken through two-way glass.

The other brothels were very comfortably furnished, with soft lighting and thick pile carpets. Clients waited for girls in a lounge and were served cocktails or coffee free of charge. All the rooms were fitted with concealed microphones, the conversations being tape-recorded by operators in the attic. From there they also took pictures in the various bedrooms, using remote controlled 35mm Olympus cameras. These were fitted with battery-powered motors that, after the shutter had been fired electrically, wound the film to the next frame. To cover up any sound from the mechanisms, the bedrooms had music piped to them.

In March 1971, this operation scored a major success when it enabled the authorities to identify the killers of three young soldiers, serving with the 1st Battalion of the Royal Highland Fusiliers, who had been shot dead on the outskirts of Belfast on March 10. Later the authorities issued a statement in which they said that complete protection had been promised to the informers who had named the killers: "We know who we are after . . . we are convinced the information we have been given is accurate, but it may prove very difficult legally to have more than circumstantial evidence."

Behind this statement lay the fact that the killers had been named by a leading figure in Belfast public life, who had been compromised into turning informer after using one of the brothels. This victim, referred to by the code name "Big Paddy," was a well-known and respected politician connected with a non-Unionist constitutional party. He was blackmailed into providing the Security Service with a number of names and addresses, some of which led to arrests. The man has since died violently.

It has also been reported that two of the girls, one from England and the other from Dublin, also died unnaturally. They were killed in London after a tour of duty in Belfast, but it has not been possible to establish a positive link between these deaths and the sexpionage operation.

The increase in intelligence reaching the Security Service was discovered by the IRA, thanks to a telephone tap they had installed on lines leading into Irish Army intelligence. The true purpose of the brothels then became clear.

One weekend in late August 1972, IRA men from London, Belfast, and Dublin met in a house on the Hill of Howth in north Dublin. The conference was presided over by the deputy director of IRA intelligence. Its purpose was to discuss ways of dealing with the sexpionage unit and another information-gathering operation which operated under the cover of a bogus cleaning service, the Four Square Laundry. The IRA men agreed to attack the laundry but were divided about what to do with the brothels. Three ideas were put forward. The first was to try to turn them to propaganda advantage by enticing some British officials into one of the brothels; members of the staff of the then Northern Ireland Secretary, William Whitelaw, were suggested as suitable victims. As soon as they came out, the house would be raided and the films seized. The photographs would then be leaked to the American and European press, with the intention of discrediting the Security Service. The second suggestion was on the same lines as the first, except that the suggested victims were members of the consular staffs of foreign governments. The third proposal was to attack and destroy both the laundry and the brothels in the same operation. After three hours of discussion it was this argument that won approval. The counterattack having been worked out in detail, the IRA men went down to the beach for an afternoon swim.

On Monday, October 2, a special-action group of IRA men and women, under orders from general headquarters, drove from Dublin to Belfast. There they collected their arms and split into two groups. One unit attacked a Four Square Laundry van in Dunmurray and killed the driver, Sapper Ted Stewart. Meanwhile, the second group had divided into two squads. One attacked the "health studio," the other the Antrim Road brothel, using pistols and sten guns. The IRA later claimed that five British agents had been killed in the operation, including the second-in-command of the brothels, a man code-named "Bossman Jim" and a girl. She was described as the daughter of a British Army brigadier, but her function in the sexpionage operation was not disclosed.

The British Army denies all these claims and says that only Ted Stewart, whom they admit was operating under cover, was killed. However, it seems certain that some type of raid was carried out on the Antrim Road establishment that Monday morning, since the road was sealed off by British troops, and equipment, said to include cameras and tape recorders, was seen being carried from the house. The IRA code-named the operation "Leo," but unofficially it became known as "Operation Dolly Fosset," an ironic tribute to a once notorious Dublin bawdyhouse.

After the raids, both the Four Square Laundry operation and the remaining brothels were closed down. Since their cover had been effectively blown, they were of no further value.

Whether the vice man's co-operation with the authorities in this strange operation, which earned him the gratitude of the Security Services, also helped him to avoid arrest is doubtful. In the long term neither his lavish bribes nor his unofficial assistance to the Crown did him much good. He was arrested and, two years after his Belfast adventures, received a six year jail sentence on vice charges, exchanging luxury for the drab discomfort of a prison cell.

British intelligence's appreciation of the value of brothels as sources of information is not of recent origin. During World War II, Winston Churchill ordered a commando raid on Nazi-occupied France in order to capture the entire staff of a German Army bordello. In late January 1944, British Army intelligence received news that the appointment of

Erwin Rommel as commander in chief of the German forces from the Netherlands to the Loire had caused Wehrmacht morale to plunge. The more fanatical young German officers, who were still convinced Nazis, were said to resent the command going to Rommel, whom they regarded as a lukewarm follower of the Führer. If this information was true, then the situation might be exploited by the Allies to weaken the German command structure in this vitally important area of Europe. The difficulty was to substantiate the report. At a conference, the British director of military intelligence remarked casually that the best judges of German officer morale were probably prostitutes in a military brothel near Lisieux. The only remaining establishment between Le Havre and Cherbourg, it had been kept open solely to serve the needs of Rommel's senior staff. "There are apparently seven girls and a madame," said the director of intelligence. Churchill chewed on his cigar for a moment. Then he growled a two-word order: "Fetch them."

This command led to what was probably the most bizarre raid of the war. In great secrecy a group of veteran commandos was assembled at a port on the south coast and briefed for the assault. They were to be landed in small boats near Lisieux while two other groups, supported by Royal Air Force bombers, made diversionary raids on either side of the target.

At first the soldiers assumed they were being sent over to abduct Rommel. When they discovered they would be snatching a group of prostitutes and an elderly brothel keeper, the briefing disintegrated into a bedlam of cheers and catcalls. After a choppy, but uneventful, crossing, the men were landed right on target. As they made their way inland, the commandos could hear the steady roar of explosions from the bombing raid. It was a moonless night in late January, and the squad encountered some difficulty in locating the château that housed the brothel. Eventually they found it and crawled cautiously through the undergrowth towards the high surrounding wall. They expected to have to scale the wall, but the iron gates stood open and unguarded. The Germans had never expected that a brothel would become a military target.

Their faces blackened, sten guns cradled in their arms, the commandos slithered forward through the shrubbery flanking the wide gravel drive. The sound of a piano drifted from the shuttered windows. By the front steps were several staff cars, their bored drivers smoking and chatting as they waited for the officers to reappear. The men were killed silently and pulled into the bushes. Then the raiders sprinted up the stone steps and crashed into the building. They ran from room to room, snatching the screaming girls from their beds and shooting down their partners. Hooded, their hands bound behind them, the seven girls and the madame were hurried along the the beach. Lamp signals flickered across the pitch-black water, and a dinghy was rowed ashore. Within two hours of being landed, the raiding party and their catch were racing back across the Channel in launches.

On arrival the girls, many of them still suffering from seasickness, were driven to London and interrogated by Military Intelligence. When they had calmed down, they confirmed the previous reports. An anti-Hitler faction amongst Rommel's staff had the support of the field marshal and General Karl Heinrich von Stülpnagel, the military governor of France. The girls remained prisoners of war until after the invasion when they were returned to France. Because of the strange and controversial nature of the raid all references to it were removed from the official history of World War II.

After the war the SIS employed prostitutes in Germany and Austria to wheedle pillow secrets from Russian soldiers, but the value of this intelligence was minimal and the British were never enthusiastic about such operations. The French, on the other hand, set considerable store by it and, according to a former British intelligence officer, there were at one time more than 400 prostitutes in the pay of French military intelligence "doing their best on their backs in the Vienna Woods."

Because of the political risks of public disclosure of such operations, the Security Service only rarely sets up entrapment brothels. If they do, such operations tend to be of limited duration and in areas where they can achieve maximum security, as in the Northern Ireland situation.

For this reason sexpionage in Britain has tended to take on a defensive rather than an offensive role. As a weapon of counterintelligence it has come under the control of the Security Service rather than the Secret Intelligence Service.

Like America, but unlike the Soviet Union, Britain has no single, esoteric, and ubiquitous intelligence service. Instead the tasks of intelligence gathering and counterintelligence security are divided between two distinct organizations. These have long, but inaccurately, been known as MI-5 and MI-6.

The abbreviations stand for "Military Intelligence," but the term is a misnomer for neither is connected with the military so far as intelligence gathering operations are concerned. All three armed services have their own intelligence units which liaise with each other and the civilian services through the defense intelligence staff. MI-6, correctly the Secret Intelligence Service (SIS), approximates the CIA. MI-5, the Security Service, is the equivalent to the FBI. The SIS is controlled by the Foreign Office and is answerable, inasmuch as it is answerable to any outsider, to the foreign secretary. The Security Service, nearly always referred to in full because of the unfortunate association their initials have with Nazi Germany, is controlled by the British Home Office.

The relationship between the Security Service and the SIS is a delicate one which often breaks down into bitter rivalry. This happened in 1969 when the Irish situation erupted. Ulster, being a part of the United Kingdom, was the responsibility of the Security Service. Southern Ireland came under the control of the SIS. Both services were quite unprepared for the hostilities and their efforts to build networks from scratch were hampered by bitter demarcation disputes.

The SIS is the largest British intelligence service and has numerous offices scattered around London. Two of its main addresses are at a hotel in Northumberland Avenue, where potential recruits are interviewed, and at 21 Queen Anne's Gate, near Buckingham Palace, where the administrative offices are located. Clandestine operations abroad are carried out by SIS officers and members of the Special Air Services, an undercover military force.

The Security Service is more centralized at Leconfield House, not far from the Hilton Hotel in Park Lane. As the service has no powers of arrest, they work in close co-operation with the police Special Branch which carries out raids and makes arrests on their behalf. The service employs only British nationals, including men and women from Northern Ireland, and is a much more military-oriented body than the SIS. All its agents are trained in both counterintelligence and counterinsurgency operations and, to keep the service at maximum fitness, the age of retirement is fifty-five.

The rivalry between the two services led, in 1962, to one of the gravest scandals ever to rock the Establishment. Called the Profumo Affair, after its best known participant, it centered around a Russian spy and a pretty call girl. Although many thousands of words have been written about the affair, the inside story of this astonishing sexpionage operation which went wrong is told here for the first time.

In January 1961, the head of the Security Service, Sir Roger Henry Hollis, called a meeting of his senior advisers. Sir Henry was an ambitious and enthusiastic intelligence officer, always more at home in an offensive rather than a defensive role. The son of the Bishop of Taunton, he was born in 1905 and went straight into the Ministry of Defense from Oxford University. In the early fifties he was sent to Australia to help set up their national security service and rapidly became involved in his first political scandal. In 1952 Vladimir Petrov, KGB spy master in Australia, defected. Among the documents he handed over to Western security officials, it was claimed, was a list of Communist agents in Australia. The Petrov list triggered a purge of government and civil-service officials which seriously damaged the Australian Labour party's chances of achieving power. Although the list may have been genuine, the suspicion remains that it was—at least in part—a Security Service forgery.

Hollis returned to England, bought an expensive house in London's fashionable Kensington, and settled down to a successful career in the service. He was awarded various honors as he rose through the ranks of counterintelligence, including a knighthood bestowed in 1960.

Despite his previous successes, when Sir Henry called together his advisers in January 1961, the tone of the conference in Leconfield House was gloomy. British security had been mauled by the press in light of the disclosures of a spy ring in the Portland weapons establishment. Not only had a major KGB spy ring been operating in the top-secret establishment for six years, but one of the key agents, Harry Houghton, had been given clearance to handle secrets when he was a known security risk. Although the spies had been caught in the end, the Security Service had come out of it badly. But their own lack of efficiency was not the major reason for the depression which characterized the January meeting. Sir Henry was angry about a major intelligence triumph by the SIS.

In 1960, the CIA in Turkey had been approached by a colonel in the Soviet military intelligence organization, the GRU, named Oleg Penkovsky. The agency investigated the colonel, decided he must be a KGB stooge, and turned down his offer of secrets. Penkovsky then called on the SIS and found them far more enthusiastic. As his work was concerned with assessing the relative merits of NATO missile capability, Penkovsky had to know a great deal about the USSR's stockpiles and research programs. It was this information he was peddling. When his value and sincerity became clear, the CIA had to go to the SIS and ask for a share in the operation. During the Cuban crisis in 1962 Penkovsky played a vital role by advising the Americans of the Soviet leadership's true intentions.

Irritated by the SIS success, Sir Henry had ordered his staff to discover an equally high-ranking Soviet operating within the UK, who might be subverted. The man they came up with was Eugene Ivanov, overtly a naval attaché at the Soviet Embassy, actually a major general in the GRU.

A thickset and rather unintelligent-looking individual, known in diplomatic circles as "Fox Face," Ivanov was in fact an experienced and brilliant spy master who had been given the task of penetrating the Portland weapons establishment. Ivanov dressed smartly and liked to spend his evenings in nightclubs. He apparently enjoyed the trappings of capitalist society and might, the Security Service felt, be prepared to sell himself if the price were right. At the January meeting it was decided to introduce the Russian to some of the more exotic trappings of British society as a prelude to subversion, and before the meeting ended the broad outlines of the sexpionage entrapment had been agreed upon.

The chosen intermediary for the Ivanov operation was a fashionable London osteopath, amateur artist, and provider of prostitutes to the Establishment, Dr. Stephen Ward. The son of a clergyman, Ward trained in his profession before the start of World War II. In 1939 he joined the Royal Army Medical Corps and in six years had risen to the rank of captain. Posted to India, he rapidly acquired social poise mixing with the British *raj*. In addition to faultless manners he possessed an ability to play bridge and an almost hypnotic charm over women, although far from handsome in the conventional sense. These attributes were to be both his making, and his breaking.

In 1947, he returned to London and started in private practice. Soon his clients included the United States ambassador, Sir Winston Churchill, Paul Getty, and Elizabeth Taylor. Ward cultivated his friends among the highest strata of society, and the lowest. He knew dukes and political leaders, but he also rubbed shoulders with gangsters, drug pushers, and prostitutes. He gained the reputation of knowing the most exciting women around. Soon the phrase "Ward girls" was being used by the influential to describe some of the prettiest prostitutes in London. In his stable were Mandy Rice-Davies and Christine Keeler, of whom Ward once remarked, "She was just an alley cat when I took her up. She wanted too much too quickly. She could have become a duchess."

His activities were well known to the Security Service, which had checked him out because of his association with senior politicians. When they needed to make use of him, to provide suitable women for visiting heads of state, they went through his friend and patron, Lord Astor.

Astor family members have always been powerful Establishment figures, active in politics, banking, commerce, and diplomacy. During the thirties, the name Cliveden, from their vast, rambling nineteenth-century mansion on the outskirts of London, became synonymous with behind-the-scenes diplomacy and political wheeling and dealing.. In earlier times Cliveden had been the setting for lavish parties and uninhibited love-making. In his *Moral Essays,* Alexander Pope condemned the second Duke of Buckingham, who squandered a fortune on building an extravagent mansion on the site, in verse: "Gallant and gay, in Cliveden's proud alcove, the bower of wanton Shrewsbury and love."

Astor was on friendly terms with senior Security Service officers and was happy to help them, and in his view his country, when asked to do so. In this case his instructions were simple. He had merely to arrange a social meeting between Ward and Ivanov. He was not told why; neither was Ward briefed about the encounter. Events were to take their natural course.

A lunch meeting was arranged and, as had been anticipated, Ward and Ivanov got on well together. Within a few weeks of that first meeting they had become friends. Ward, a gifted artist who had sketched several members of the Royal family, asked if he might sketch Ivanov, and the Russian agreed. In return Ward introduced him to attractive women and invited him down to stay at a cottage on the Cliveden estate which he rented from Lord Astor for a nominal sum.

On Sunday, July 9, Ward's party at the cottage included Ivanov and Christine Keeler. Towards dusk they decided to go for a swim in Astor's outdoor pool, which was situated close to the main house. Lord Astor was also entertaining guests that weekend, amongst them Secretary of State for War John Profumo and his wife.

After dinner his Lordship suggested a stroll around the grounds, and his party wandered towards the walled pool. Intrigued by sounds of laughter, Lord Astor pushed open the gate in the high wall and ushered his guests through at the precise moment Christine Keeler emerged, naked, from the pool. John Profumo, walking ahead of the others, "must have seen every detail of Christine," Ward commented afterwards. "And there was a lot to see."

It was the start of a relationship between the girl and the war minister that was to have disastrous consequences for both Profumo's career and Sir Henry Hollis's subversion operation.

The fact that John Profumo and Christine Keeler were having an affair soon became known to the Security Service. There was some discussion of using the minister to help subvert Ivanov, but it was decided that this would be far too politically dangerous. Instead, a senior Security Service official was sent to see Profumo and warn him to stay away from Christine. His delicate hints were completely misunderstood by the minister. The man was trying to tell him, without actually saying so, that he had stumbled into a secret operation. It seems likely that John Profumo merely thought he was being reminded of a possible scandal if he continued to see Christine. If he did think this, it made no difference to his relationship with the young woman, for by this time he was too infatuated with her to worry about any threat it posed to his career. Hollis, unable to prevent Profumo from seeing Keeler, concentrated on Ivanov's defection.

Every delight that London society could offer was strewn in the KGB man's path. Outwardly Ivanov seemed to be captivated by his new social life. In fact, he was well aware of the subversion attempt and had reported every meeting back to Moscow from his first lunch with Ward. At first the KGB ordered Ivanov to play along with the Security Service because, through Ward, he would be able to infiltrate many useful areas of the Establishment. But within a few months of the first meeting with Ward, and before the Profumo encounter, Ivanov had discovered another good reason for staying close to the osteopath. In his friend's London flat, the Russian discovered a two-way mirror. Ward had not installed this device; it was put there by a previous owner. But he had used it to watch his friends making love and to take numerous photographs. From the negatives he produced three sets of prints and had them bound into albums.* Ivanov knew that this material would offer magnificent material for blackmail. He secretly copied the more valuable pictures and sent them to Moscow. Today they are on file at Dzerzhinsky Square awaiting the opportune moment to be used.

Profumo's affair with Christine Keeler made the Ward setup of even greater interest to the Russians, and Ivanov was ordered to take any steps necessary to subvert the war minister. Such was Ivanov's devotion

---

*One of these albums was seized from the flat by the police, a second confiscated from a friend of Ward's. The third has never been located.

to duty that the heterosexual Soviet even went to bed with one of Christine Keeler's bisexual boy friends in the hope of gaining information.

On December 14, 1962, one of Christine Keeler's boy friends went to Ward's Wimpole Mews flat and fired shots into the building. His jealous rage caused the simmering scandal to explode onto the front pages of the press. Fleet Street had known about Profumo's association with a call girl for months, but hadn't dared to print a word of it. Now they splashed the sensational story.

Sir Henry kept his nerve right up to the end, praying for the defection which would justify the whole operation. He refused to believe that there had been any risk of information leaking to the Russians from Profumo's liaison, a view which was certainly correct. But events were now beyond his control. On June 6 Ward was arrested, and at the end of July he killed himself with a drug overdose. A few months later Sir Henry was forced to retire from his $16,000-a-year job. He moved to Crossway Cottage near the West Country town of Bridgewater and spent his last years growing roses, an embittered old man who believed he had been shabbily treated by a country he had served faithfully for more than forty years. Profumo resigned from his seat in Parliament and slipped into obscurity, working for charities and visiting prisons. Christine Keeler married in 1971, but separated from her husband a year later.

In October 1973, Sir Henry Hollis died. For two days his cottage was the scene of uncharacteristic activity as Special Branch officers searched it painstakingly behind drawn curtains. It is believed they were looking for any tapes or manuscript notes the spy master might have left behind: a last message to the world in place of the biography which he had been forbidden to write, an explanation of the true facts of a sexpionage trap which went wrong because a minister of the Crown blundered into a naked prostitute.

Ivanov went back to Moscow during the scandal and is now a top-rank GRU officer, his loyalty never doubted by the party. With hindsight the attempted subversion may seem naive, but almost identical operations carried out since then have proved successful. Less than ten years after the attempted Ivanov entrapment, for example, the Security Service was able to persuade KGB illegal Oleg Lyalin to defect.

Lyalin arrived in Britain in 1969 with the cover of a trade official with the Soviet trade delegation based in Highgate, north London. As a KGB officer attached to the Scientific and Technical Department, Directorate T, of the First Chief Directorate, thirty-two-year-old Lyalin was to help co-ordinate industrial espionage against Britain. This assignment didn't prove to be a difficult task. Following the signing of a trade agreement between the UK and USSR, British manufacturers were keen to enter the lucrative new marketplace. Visiting Soviets were given conducted tours of factories and laboratories in the hope of encouraging sales. Even items on the Board of Trade's list of goods subject to security control, which could only be exported under special license, were available for inspection.

The Security Service soon identified Lyalin not only as a KGB agent but as a potential defector. A married man whose family was in Russia, he was involved with his secretary, Mrs. Irina Teplyakova. The Security Service managed to steer the couple into a sexpionage entrapment and obtained photographs. At the same time Lyalin was being encouraged, through British friends, to enjoy the "glamorous" West. He began to drink heavily. In August 1971, he was stopped by two policemen while driving his Hillman saloon erratically. An alcohol test proved positive and the Russian was arrested. Lyalin had no diplomatic immunity to protect him and he knew he would have to appear in court and face immediate return to Russia after the case. At this crossroad in his life the Security Service presented him with the photographic evidence and offered a deal. In return for his defection and details of the Soviet spy ring, they would offer lifetime protection for himself and Irina Teplyakova. He accepted. As a result a major KGB network was smashed and some 105 Russian officials were expelled for espionage and sabotage.

A far more routine use of sexpionage in Britain is for defensive operations. Visiting heads of state and other VIPs who want to sleep with a pretty girl are helped to do so in such a way that there is no risk of their being blackmailed or catching VD. During the sixties the Security Service ran a brothel for this purpose in Church Street, Kensington. The brothel was housed in a number of private apartments and was elegantly furnished and staffed by attractive and experienced prostitutes. Every girl had been investigated by the Special Branch prior to employment and each one received regular medical inspections. Clients, who were given the address by Foreign Office or Board of Trade officials, never realized they were being directed to a Security Service-controlled brothel. They paid for the girls in the normal way and the high prices charged made the establishment profitable. It was closed down in 1969 for fear of press disclosure.

Today suitable women are still available to important visitors, but the cost of the service is met out of the British government's hospitality fund. This fund, which takes some $700,000 from the UK taxpayer each year, is specifically for the entertainment of overseas guests. The only hospitality officially provided includes such distractions as receptions, chauffeur-driven limousines, tickets to football games, and seats at the opera. The Foreign Office denies that any of the money goes towards procuring prostitutes; nevertheless, it does.

One of the women used to find suitable call girls for this service was Irish-born Norma Russell, herself a prostitute with many eminent government officials among her clients. They included Lord Lambton, parliamentary under-secretary of state for defense for the Royal Air Force, and Lord Jellicoe, leader of the House of Lords. She selected suitable girls and passed their names to the Foreign Office, who forwarded them to the Security Service. The girls were investigated for security purposes and then given a medical examination. If accepted, they went on a Foreign Office list of suitable escorts for VIPs. Sometimes the girls were supplied on request and there was no pretense that they were other than high-class prostitutes. On other occasions a more subtle game was played. The women acted the roles of secretaries or receptionists and allowed the VIP in question to apparently pick them up. The idea was that the visitor would be so delighted with his skill in charming an attractive young woman into bed that he would be more receptive to whatever proposals of a political or commercial nature were put to him. The girls received about $100 a time, though Norma Russell, or Levy, as she called herself, charged more. She held the leases on two expensive apartments in one of the most fashionable areas of London. Her references included letters from a millionaire, a firm of stockbrokers, and a bank.

The Norma Levy network was dispersed after news of her relationship with Lord Lambton became public. In the bedroom of one of her apartments was a two-way mirror through which Norma's permanent boy friend had taken pictures of her with clients. He attempted to sell these to the British press. The newspaper accounts emphasized the security risks: the boy friend, they argued, might just as easily have offered his pictures to the Russians. No doubt the Security Service appreciated the irony of being charged with the very mistake their call-girl system was designed to prevent. Commenting on the idea of providing visiting VIPs with prostitutes who will neither attempt to blackmail them nor give them venereal disease, Marcus Lipton, the Labour MP for Brixton, probably summed up the unspoken attitude of most Western governments when he commented, "Everyone knows that this sort of thing goes on, especially with exchange visits of MPs and diplomats from countries whose social standards are slightly different from our own. They expect facilities to be provided."

10

Invasion of the Bedrooms

In September 1964, Horst Schwirkmann, one of West Germany's top debugging experts, was called to Moscow to make a routine sweep of the West German Embassy for electronic listening devices. It was a trick for which the electronics expert was especially adept. Not only a brilliant engineer, Schwirkmann had the uncanny knack of being able to think himself into the minds of the Soviet bugging teams and outwit them at every turn. On one occasion he playfully rigged up a device which sent a high-frequency sound into the microphones he had just discovered. The result was that the KGB's receiving equipment was severely damaged and their agents got a mammoth headache—literally. Schwirkmann and his colleagues enjoyed the joke tremendously, but it did little to endear him to the KGB. During his routine visit to Moscow in September the Soviets decided to get him back. Schwirkmann swept the embassy with his "fumigation" equipment, locating and destroying a dozen KGB microphones. So efficiently did he work that the whole building had been electronically cleaned two days ahead of schedule. Schwirkmann, who carried a diplomatic passport identifying him as a third secretary in the commercial department, decided to spend his free time sight-seeing. On his last Sunday, he drove with five other Germans from the embassy to visit the ancient Troitsko-Sergeyev monastery at Zagorsk, forty-five miles from Moscow. With other tourists, the Germans wandered around the fourteenth-century masterpiece, admiring the magnificent collection of art treasures, the icons and silver ornaments, the elaborate wood carvings, and the hand-painted books. At one point a man brushed close to Schwirkmann and, when the man had gone, the German felt that his left trouser leg was slightly damp. It seemed curious, but no more than that. As they left the building the Germans met a gray-bearded monk who offered to show them around the old town of Zagorsk. Schwirkmann was enthusiastic, but his five colleagues wanted to get back to the embassy. So they politely declined the offer and started the hour-long drive back to Moscow. It was a decision which was to save Schwirkmann's life. On the ride home he started to feel sick. By the time their car pulled up outside the embassy he was semi-conscious and moaning in agony.

They carried him to an upstairs room where a hastily summoned American doctor diagnosed severe mustard gas burns. He told the anxious German ambassador, "This man must go to hospital immediately or he may die."

The embassy security staff was faced with a difficult decision. If Schwirkmann went to the hospital, it was possible that the Russians would use drugs or other interrogation methods to extract valuable information about the secret techniques used to detect and neutralize their listening devices.

The risk of allowing him to go to the hospital for treatment was considered too great. It was decided to fly him back to Bonn and hope he would survive the journey. But when the embassy tried to book an early flight out of Moscow, an Intourist official told them there were no seats available. For forty-eight hours the deadly game went on while Schwirkmann's life hung in the balance. Finally, the pressure from West Germany and her allies became so intense that the Russians relented. Space on an aircraft suddenly became available and Schwirkmann was flown to Bonn, where he received treatment at the university clinic There experts discovered that his leg had been sprayed with a type of powerful mustard gas. Slowly the electronics expert recovered and, when he was finally able to leave the hospital, the West German secret service paid him substantial compensation for his sufferings.

At the time Schwirkmann was attacked, the art of bugging was still a relatively crude affair. Radio-microphones, although increasingly small, were still based on transistor circuits with soldered components and circuits etched onto copper silica. By using extremely tiny components, technicians were able to reduce circuits to sizes which were regarded as amazing. Radio transmitters could be built inside cocktail olives—the stick provided the aerial—and fitted into sugar cubes. These techniques caught the imagination of press and public alike. At the time they seemed the last word in electronic sophistication. Today they appear as crude as a World War I crystal set.

Although it has lagged behind the CIA in micro-circuit technology, the KGB has always been interested in subminiature radio-microphones and cigarette-packet-sized tape recorders. In 1969, KGB technicians managed to bug the left shoe of the American ambassador in Bucharest. The opportunity arose when the embassy maid took the shoes to a local cobbler for repair. While the shoes were being resoled, a technician inserted a tiny transmitting device, powered by five mercury cells, into a hollowed-out heel. Two small holes were drilled on the front edge of the heels and these were used to switch the bug on and off. Each morning the maid would insert a pin through one of the holes to switch the equipment on, and every evening she pushed a pin into the other hole to switch it off. The bug operated successfully and might have gone on doing so for months if a security officer hadn't detected its transmission during a routine fumigation sweep of the embassy. As he turned on his high-frequency monitoring equipment, the officer was astonished to hear the ambassador's voice discussing business with a senior diplomat. Horrified, he raced into the ambassador's office and handed him a note warning him that he was on the air.

For every success they chalked up, these early gadgets produced an equal number of failures, sometimes embarrassing failures. On one occasion in 1955, an American agent in Berlin was meeting his opposite number for an informal, strictly off-the-record discussion. Suddenly the agent's tape recorder, which was wired to a microphone concealed in his wrist watch, began to screech alarmingly. As one of the conditions of their meeting had been that no tapes would be carried, it looked as though their carefully arranged meeting would end abruptly. The DDR agent stared at his colleague for a long while as the screeching got louder. Finally he asked him, apologetically, "Do you think, Herr ———, that your tape recorder has gone wrong, or is it mine?"

The real breakthrough in electronic espionage came in the late sixties with the perfection of micro-electronic "chip" circuits. These are complete circuits built up on tiny wafers of silicon. At first, these pinhead-sized circuits were costly and difficult to produce, but today they can be cheaply mass-produced. It was by using a chip transmitter that the CIA was able to produce, experimentally, what must be considered the ultimate bug: a .25-centimeter diameter radio microphone fixed to the back of a house fly. This astonishing gadget was first reported in *El-Djeich*, the monthly magazine of the Algerian armed forces, in 1973. According to the writer, the flies could be used to carry their transmitters into heavily guarded and stringently screened conference rooms by way of the keyholes and ventilation systems. Before being sent out on its mission, the fly would be given a whiff of nerve gas which would kill it within a predetermined period of time. Soon after reaching its target area the fly would collapse, thus enabling the transmitter to operate without being deafened by the buzzing of wings.

If this seems like science fiction run riot, another bugging gadget under development by the CIA in the early 1970s was a radio transmitter flown onto bedroom windowsills by specially trained pigeons. Powerful but lightweight transmitters were fitted onto the pigeons, who were guided to the right room by means of a red laser beam aimed at the appropriate window. Having obediently followed the beam and alighted on the sill, the pigeons pecked at a button that released the transmitter, which was then automatically activated. The mission completed, the pigeon flew back to base.

It is unlikely that the KGB, lacking the CIA's total dedication to gadgetry, has been experimenting along these lines. Usually they are content to fix up love nests with permanent bugs and cameras and then maneuver victims into their web. In sexpionage, hidden microphones serve two main functions. They enable bedroom conversations to be recorded and, occasionally, useful secrets are let slip by indiscreet lovers. Far more frequently eavesdropping is carried out to let the agents know the right moment to switch on the cameras or put their shoulders to the door. Getting the timing right is of paramount importance and has led to the development of a wide range of ingenious gadgets.

In the late sixties, an electronic pill was developed as an aid to medical research into digestion. It was an aspirin-sized radio transmitter which the patient swallowed. As it passed through the body, the doctor could monitor the signal and extract important information about the stomach and intestines. Both the Russians and the Americans experimented with these pills for several months, although it is not known if they ever went into general use. The KGB felt that the pills would make surveillance far easier and more certain. If a person has been trained to detect and throw off a tail, it becomes virtually impossible to follow him. During a number of experiments the KGB made the swallow take the radio pill along with her contraceptive pill and then practiced following her and the target electronically. The CIA, too, used radio pills as an aid to surveillance.

The experiments seem to have been successful because the KGB next tried to find ways of making the target swallow a radio pill as well, so that they could accurately pinpoint the moment when the couple had sex. The pills were tuned to slightly different frequencies. While the bodies containing them were apart, each signal could be clearly heard. When, in the words of one CIA man, "navel engagement" was achieved, the signals merged into one. It is doubtful if this idea ever caught on, as the problems of persuading a victim to swallow a radio pill must be considerable. The stomach is by no means the most intimate place in which transmitters have been located. One has been designed to fit on the breast and another, which I shall describe a little later, built to insert into the vagina.

The breast transmitter, developed by an American corporation, was fitted into a fake nipple. This was intended not for entrapment work but for female undercover agents who might want to be wired for sound, in such a way that not even the most intimate naked body search could betray the transmitter. First a cast is taken in plaster of both nipples and these are then moulded in a fine, flesh-colored rubber. Because the fake nipple protrudes a fraction of a centimeter above the real nipple, it is necessary to equip a woman with a pair to prevent her from appearing asymmetric. The radio equipment, which can be fitted into either nipple, consists of a circular chip transmitter with a microphone which picks up sounds coming through fine perforations in the rubber. Ingeniously powered by body heat, it is said to have a range of several hundred feet. An equally cunning hiding place for transmitters, which has been used by both the Russians and the Americans, is inside a false tooth. Here again espionage has borrowed from medical research. The radio tooth was originally developed for dental investigation, a molar being equipped with a transmitter, aerial, batteries, and sensors which measured the stress involved in chewing. The radio tooth is mainly used to enable undercover agents to report back without the risk of a wire being discovered.

With the advent of ultra-minute TV cameras and video-tape recording equipment, many of the KGB's problems in photographing entrapments were solved. Before then all entrapments had to be recorded on photographic emulsion. Kodak developed an ultra-high-speed film for surveillance work, Kodak recording film, but even this emulsion needs a level of illumination which is high compared with the sensitivity of electronic equipment. The alternative to shooting pictures on fast films, using available light, was to flood the scene with infrared light and use a special emulsion and filters. Although infrared light is invisible to the human eye, it is still possible to spot the dull ruby-red glow of the light source.

When still cameras are used, a popular model for sexpionage entrapments is the Japanese-designed Nikon. This is a single-lens reflex camera taking standard 35mm film either in casettes holding thirty-six exposures, or in bulk-loading packs which take sufficient film to give 250 exposures. The Nikons are fitted with electric motors, powered by batteries, which take a picture and automatically advance the film. The motor allows the camera to be operated by remote control. According to the motor setting, the camera will either take single pictures slowly or fire a sequence of shots at up to four pictures a second. The chief difficulty in using motorized Nikons is the noise they make. Quite complicated soundproofing is essential to prevent the target hearing the camera firing and winding the film. The noise can be limited by modifications to the shutter system and by locking the reflex mirror, which normally travels up and down as a picture is taken. Even with these adaptations, a soundproof blimp is still needed. This increases the size of an already bulky camera considerably. A motorized Nikon with blimp is about eighteen inches square, although the aperture through which the picture is taken is only an inch in diameter. Because these cameras must be loaded with film before an operation and emptied again soon afterwards, easy access to the equipment must be provided. This can be arranged by drilling through a wall in a hotel bedroom and keeping the bulk of the camera on the opposite side. The lens opening may be hidden behind a picture with a tiny hole punched in the canvas or a two-way mirror. Alternatively the camera can be positioned above the bed by cutting through from the room above. In this position the lens opening is usually hidden by painting the ceiling a dark color or by elaborate plaster molding. This position is less frequently used for a number of reasons. It is harder to obtain satisfactory heterosexual entrapment pictures when the subjects are having sex in the normal "missionary" position, as the man's face tends to be obscured. Only if the woman is taking the active role does the camera location yield satisfactory material. There are technical problems too: a room with an overhead light may cause flare in the lens which will reduce the image quality Thus one of the most effective positions is slightly above and to one side of the bed, with the camera angled down. Swallows are always aware of the camera location and, as we have seen, are trained to position their companions in order to produce the most convincing pictures.

The main difficulty in using still cameras is knowing when to start them running. With only limited film stock available, even on 250-exposure loadings, there is the risk of the camera running out at the crucial moment. Only in a few situations is it possible for an operator to be present behind the camera to watch the action and start taking pictures at the most appropriate moment.

One simple technique by which an operator can observe and take photographs is to use a single-lens reflex camera fitted to an optical fiber device. Optical fibers are hair-thin, flexible glass rods which will guide light waves around corners. Here again sexpionage owes a debt to medical research, because this system was first developed to enable surgeons to examine and operate inside patients without cutting them open. A fine tube carrying a light source and a bundle of fibers is pushed down the sedated patient's throat into the stomach, intestines, or lungs. The doctor can then make a diagnosis, or take photographs. Optical fibers have been used experimentally by the KGB in oder to take pictures through keyholes or to bring an image into a nearby room. The quality is said to be good provided a sufficiently sophisticated optical system is used.

Before looking at some of the systems which have been devised to overcome the problems of activating automatic cameras at the right moment, we should deal briefly with movie films. These are only occasionally used in sexpionage because of the limitations of such films as compromising material. It is far more effective for an agent to hand his victim a batch of incriminating glossy photographs than to invite him to a viewing theater and run a projector. Targets are more afraid of prints which, sent through the mail to wives or employers, are instantly damning. Of course movie film has an important part to play in espionage. For one thing, it is a far more effective method of training agents to identify a target than still photographs. A film shows not merely what the man or woman looks like, but how they walk, what identifying gestures they make and how they react to their environment. It might be thought that a movie camera, containing many hundred feet of film, would be very suitable for entrapment work. Why not shoot the activity on 16mm film and then take prints from the appropriate frames? The difficulty is that most film cameras operate at a fairly slow shutter speed, typically around 1/60th of a second. This means that movement will be blurred on a still photograph. When the stock has been processed for maximum speed, the print can become so indistinct and grainy that features are not clearly identifiable, and so the whole object of the entrapment is lost.

When a still camera has to be set up to operate automatically, a number of gadgets can be used. The simplest is a fine cable, concealed by carpet or under the floorboards, running from the camera position to a micro-switch fastened beneath the bed springs. The switch is adjusted so that it closes under the weight of two people resting on the bed, but remains in the "off" position when only one person is on the bed. In theory this system would seem to be foolproof. The KGB has used it in conjunction with a timing device which, once the switch has been closed, takes a picture every fifteen to twenty seconds. In practice it has proved less satisfactory than was hoped. Adjusting the micro-switch pressure is far from easy, even when the weight of the swallow is known in advance. Early experiments produced dozens of pictures of the nude swallow lying on the bed while the target sat fully clothed beside her pulling off his shoes. Furthermore, the wire connection and the micro-switch were easily detected by the victim. If he discovered the device he would most probably run a mile; alternatively he might impudently render the entrapment useless by cutting the cable. To overcome the second problem the cable was replaced by a radio transmitter fitted to the micro-switch, the whole unit being concealed inside a mattress. The pressure sensor, too, was improved by KGB technicians until it became so sensitive and discriminating that two people sitting on the bed, or even bouncing up and down, failed to trigger the camera, while the specific movements of intercourse set it running.

But while this system proved satisfactory on the majority of occasions, it failed to take into account man's sexual ingenuity. Vera, the swallow whose story I told in Chapter Four, told me that on occasion her targets insisted on making love on the floor, with her bending over an armchair, and even in the bath. The only common denominator in such a situation is the woman herself, and ways were sought to enable her to trigger the automatic camera. The most extraordinary piece of equipment constructed for this task was a thumbnail-sized vaginal transmitter which was said to be as easy to fit and as comfortable to wear as the coil contraceptive. The transmitter is triggered by chemical changes in the vagina during intercourse and starts the camera turning. This device was completely satisfactory except when the swallow got a target who insisted on oral or anal intercourse—special adaptations were no doubt considered!

Most of these elaborate triggering systems were made obsolete by the development of the miniature TV camera, the light intensifying tube, and the video-tape recorder which are now used in the majority of KGB entrapments.

In 1972, the Radio Corporation of American announced the development of the, then, world's smallest television camera. It measured 2" × 2¼" × 3¾" and weighed less than one pound. After undergoing tests at the American Air Force laboratory in Ohio, the camera went into production for a number of surveillance projects, including satellite work. The small size of this camera was made possible by using integrated circuits instead of vacuum tubes. The electronics included a so-called "bucket brigade" circuit, named because bits of the image are transferred from one element to the next like water being passed down a human fire-fighting chain. Since then, work in CIA and KGB laboratories has still further reduced the size of such equipment. Exactly how much further it is impossible to say because all such research is a closely guarded secret.

An equally stringent security screen hides the development of light-intensification lenses. These function by taking what light is available and amplifying it electronically to many thousands of times its original brightness. An intensification tube has three stages and light passing from one stage to the next is massively increased. For this reason the system is known as the "three-stage cascade." In the first section, light falling on a sensitive photo-cathode produces a stream of electrons. These are accelerated and transformed into visible light energy, a procedure which is repeated in each of the stages. Power, from a cell not much larger than a household battery, is stepped up to produce brief discharges of 45,000 volts. Equipment of this type has been under development for many years at the Signal Research and Development Establishment at Christchurch in Hampshire, England. Here they have constructed a complex test tunnel in which any lighting conditions from pitch darkness to moonlight or the illumination from a few stars, can be duplicated. Using this equipment under "starlight conditions," it is possible to clearly see a target image at the end of the 100-yard-long tunnel.

In the laboratories of Rank Precision Instruments in England, I was shown an intensification unit built into a large-aperture telephoto lens. This enables an operator to observe and photograph distant objects by starlight. Another British firm, Pilkington Perkin-Elmer, part of the Pilkington Glass group, has developed a nine-pound instrument which can detect an object a meter in length at a distance of nearly one mile—by starlight; called the Lolite, it retails at over $3,500.

Using such intensifiers it is possible to take pictures by the glow of a cigarette. During one test, objects two miles away were photographed by the equivalent of a 100-watt household bulb.

Light-intensifying lenses have a wide range of application in military, police, and espionage operations. Some indication of the seriousness with which the West is taking such research can be judged from the general belief that in the last five years America has spent at least $100 million on this project alone.

What does a typical KGB entrapment setup look like today? Let us imagine the scene on a Moscow night as the subject and a swallow enter his hotel bedroom. They start to undress. The room is illuminated only by a shaded bedside light. Naked, they embrace and lie down on the bed. The swallow flings aside the coverlet and sheet; not even modern equipment can film or photograph through opaque material. The bedroom appears just like any other, comfortable, warm, private. But it is an electronic nightmare designed to capture the most intimate moments of their love-making. Let us suppose that the room is equipped with a completely automatic system. It will then be criss-crossed by an invisible network of ultra-sonic beams. These are linked to a small computer which monitors the frequency and pattern with which the beams are broken. A single person walking around the room will produce a different sequence than a couple moving about. The gadget decides that there are two people present and starts the camera running. There are two cameras in the room, each covering the bed from a different angle. They are hidden in the walls and are taking their pictures through specially coated glass whose front surfaces can be made to match the color of the walls. Only the most careful search would reveal their presence. The cameras have light-intensification tubes which enable them to operate by starlight if necessary. As they are switched on, built-in photo sensors measure the available light and adjust the sensitivity of the equipment to safeguard the tubes. The images are fed to briefcase-sized video-tape recorders located in the same building or, conceivably, miles away. The entire system operates without any supervision. All the KGB agent has to do the next morning is to pick up the casette of inch-wide recording tape. Still photographs can then be taken in the laboratories from appropriate sections.

If the cameras were being manually adjusted, then an operator could switch them on at the right moment and control them from a monitor. He might take pictures on a still camera directly from this screen, or merely observe the couple and adjust the camera. By using zoom lenses fitted with servomotors, the agent could pull back for a wide-angle view of the whole bedroom, or zero in for a close-up. He might be located in the hotel basement, in a nearby bedroom, in an office at Dzerzhinsky Square, or even in another city. Distance is no obstacle for the modern sex spy.

This may sound like the ultimate form of electronic voyeurism, but it seems certain that the technological assault on the privacy of the bedroom has only just started. Advances in television design will soon make it possible to produce a camera so small that it can be planted as quickly and simply as the present-day dime-sized radio microphone. Laser beams may be used to collect visual as well as aural information from distant rooms. By the year 2001, it might be possible for intelligence officers, sitting in control centers hundreds of miles from their targets, to press a switch and tune in to the activities in any room of any building.

Perhaps even more terrifying is the possible use of drugs to cut down the amount of time at present required to manipulate victims into sexpionage entrapments. Even with an eager and sexually uninhibited subject, this can take a few days. From the spy master's point of view it would be far more satisfactory if, within a few minutes of their meeting, the target and swallow, or raven, could be making love Experiments now being carried out at the University of California at San Diego suggest some ways in which this might be achieved Researchers there have found ways of adjusting the personality by means of small doses of drugs. In one experiment a mild, shy man who might be expected to be inhibited in the company of women was made to behave confidently and even aggressively after taking a small quantity of an amphetamine derivative. In another experiment a female volunteer who was known to be a devoted and dependent wife was, temporarily, changed into a self-centered person after being given an antidepressant drug.

Dr Arnold Mandell, who carried out many of the experiments in the university's medical school, commented: "The important thing to realize is that with our knowledge we can now create any mental life style we want. What is 'normal' becomes a manipulative tool."

There are a number of ways in which such drugs could be used in sexpionage entrapments. Suppose, for example, that a Western scientist with vital secrets locked away in his brain visits the Soviet Union to attend a conference. One evening he is discreetly doped and a swallow is maneuvered into his company. Previously too uncertain of himself to have accepted her advances, the drug has made him bold, passionate, and uninhibited. They go to his room and make love. The following day, the effects of the drug having worn off, the horrified scientist is confronted with the evidence of his sexual violence. Stunned, unable to believe he was capable of such behavior but forced to accept the fact that he had done so, the guilty and shattered man is in no position to fight back. He agrees to co-operate with the KGB, and a spy is born.

Alternatively, a happily married woman, devoted to her family, might have these deep emotional ties temporarily severed by means of drugs. Her behavior having been adjusted, she is introduced to a raven. They have an affair and compromising material is collected. With the drug removed, she is disgusted with herself and terrified that it might damage her marriage. She, too, agrees to turn traitor.

Even with a confident and uninhibited man or woman the drugs could be useful in speeding up an entrapment. With all normal social restraints removed, the KGB prostitute could easily lure the victim into bed without having to waste time in building up a relationship between them. A few drops of the right chemical and the unsuspecting man or woman would be transformed into the willing accomplice of his or her own destruction.

11

Safeguarding Our Secrets

Queen Victoria, when asked what missionary ladies shoud do if threatened with rape, is supposed to have answered: "Cross their legs and think of the Empire!"

Apocryphal or not, that regal exhortation is about as practical as much of the advice currently being handed out by the security services to potential sexpionage victims. A British design engineer making his first trip to Moscow told me how he was summoned to a small room in the Foreign Office a week before his departure and given a vague warning about possible KGB subversion techniques. "The official was slightly embarrassed," the engineer recalled. "His manner was a bit like a father telling his son the facts of life. Only in this case all he said was that pretty girls might be directed across my path during a visit to the Soviet Union and that I might, possibly, feel like going to bed with them. His only piece of advice if this happened was—'don't.'"

This case is typical. Businessmen, scientists, journalists, diplomats, and others intending to visit or work in Soviet-bloc countries are seldom sufficiently briefed about the risks they will run. Vague and general warnings take the place of detailed information about the scope and sophistication of KGB sexpionage techniques.

Many I spoke to had the impression the worst that would happen was that an attractive woman might get friendly in a bar or restaurant and try to persuade them to go to bed. Few realized how subtle and complicated entrapments could be or understood that the KGB is prepared to invest limitless time, effort, and money to snare a really important victim.

In an age when mankind walks a tightrope across the chasm of nuclear destruction men and women with secrets worth stealing must be given the maximum possible protection. Even more important, perhaps, those in positions of authority, whether political, economic, industrial, or scientific, must be safeguarded against possible subversion. There is still a tendency to think of espionage only in terms of actually collecting information. Certainly this is still an important element of spying, though less so than it used to be. Secrets tend to have a short life these days, and what is highly sensitive material today may be valueless a month from now. Military equipment becomes obsolete, on occasion, even before it goes into service; codes and ciphers can be changed swiftly; defense planning is flexible enough to survive even major breaches of security. But a man or woman subverted and then allowed to go free to continue a career is like a time bomb ticking away within the very core of society—a bomb that can be detonated, at the most damaging moment, by remote control from 2 Dzerzhinsky Square.

These twin factors of spying and subversion are what, ultimately, make sexpionage a greater menace to peace and security than all the satellites, spy planes, and spy ships together.

How can our secrets be safeguarded? How can a successful counterattack be mounted against a technique that manipulates men and women at such an intimate and psychologically complex level?

The ideal answer would be to neutralize the majority of entrapments by removing the blackmail basis on which they depend. For example, before homosexual behavior between consenting adults in private was legalized in England and Wales, scores of men found themselves the victims of blackmailers each year. Since the passing of that act, in 1967, the scope for such extortioners has been drastically curtailed.

As for sexpionage, legal changes are unlikely to make any difference, since, in many cases, it is not fear of the law but of social disgrace, marital breakup, or professional ruin that leads victims to collaborate with the KGB. However, changes in social attitudes towards sexual behavior would have a profound and valuable effect in limiting the power of such entrapments. If Western society could accept that sexual behavior between willing adults, even behavior that some might term deviant, was a matter that concerned nobody but those involved, it would have come a long way towards neutralizing sexpionage. Some security breaches would still occur, of course. No change in public opinion will safeguard a frustrated and lonely spinster from the advances of an attentive and attractive raven, nor prevent a man with secrets from becoming infatuated with a beautiful swallow. These risks would have to be dealt with in other ways.

It might be argued that most European countries and the United States have already moved far towards achieving this more liberal and laissez-faire attitude. To an extent this is true. But behavior acceptable as normal in the average citizen is still, apparently, regarded with horror when performed by those in public life. In Britain, in the early sixties, John Profumo, an able, intelligent, and sensitive man, was driven from office and publicly pilloried because of his association with Christine Keeler. More than a decade later, in what many regard as one of the world's more permissive societies, another valuable public servant, Lord Lambton, was forced to resign for similar reasons. Yet he had done only what most of his fellow citizens could have done with impunity—gone to bed with an attractive woman who was not his wife.

Perhaps in such cases the indignation that members of the public are supposed to feel is more apparent than real. Self-righteous leaders, coupled with banner headlines and as much sensational detail as can be dredged up, sell newspapers and make interesting reading.

But it is the threat of just such exposure, exactly this type of public humiliation and disgrace, that persuades many sexpionage victims to turn traitor in the hope of salvaging their dignity and their careers. Whilst I would be the last to deny the public the right to information about matters of legitimate interest, there is no doubt that many exposé stories featuring sexpionage victims provide valuable ammunition to the faceless men of Dzerzhinsky Square.

All changes in social attitude take time. The kind of changes needed to render the majority of sexpionage entrapments valueless would have to be so massive that this solution may never become a practical reality What other steps then might be taken? From the point of view of the authorities, I believe the following changes are urgently needed on both sides of the Atlantic.

1. There should be an amnesty for all sexpionage victims, even if their subversion has led to actual breaches in security. They should be encouraged to inform their security services about how, when, and where the entrapments took place. Full disclosures of this nature would undoubtedly lead to the breaking up of many professionally run KGB networks throughout the West. Furthermore, many hundreds of men and women would have an enormous burden of guilt and fear lifted from

their shoulders. These unwilling accomplices of the KGB could once again resume their rightful place in society.

2. Those who have been trapped by sexpionage operation should be encouraged to tell the authorities immediately so that steps can be taken to remove them from danger. This will require a change of outlook on the part of the authorities, including the security services, who frequently treat men and women involved in entrapments as the villains rather than the victims. Such an understanding will have to include those whose entrapment has involved deviant sexual behavior, however distasteful such activities may be to the authorities. For instance, homosexual behavior should not be penalized by dismissal, since it is the fear of such a sanction, and not the nature of their sexuality, that makes homosexuals especially vulnerable to sexpionage.

3. The amount of material presently classified as secret should be drastically reduced. Most security experts agree that far too many documents are currently being stamped secret or top secret. It often seems that the main reason for doing this is not that the material is highly sensitive but that it serves a bureaucratic convenience, protects officials from embarrassing disclosure of blunders, or inflates the importance of inadequate reports. On one occasion, for instance, the SIS purchased some copies of a British magazine that had a detailed article on Warsaw Pact defenses. The material was photocopied for distribution around the various departments and every copy was stamped "Secret"!

The consequence of overextensive classifying is not more, but less, real security. In Germany, for example, the MfS, working as the Trojan horse of the KGB, uses such excessive secrecy to hamper seriously the work of the Federal counterintelligence agencies. By recruiting thousands of agents throughout the Republic and then using them to track down trivial secrets, the MfS enables top-flight professional spies to operate more easily and safely. While counterintelligence men are occupied hunting the petty criminals of the espionage world, spies of the caliber of Yevgeny Runge and, more recently, Guenter Guillaume (aide to former Federal Chancellor Willy Brandt) can avoid detection for years.

By reducing the number of documents that have to be guarded, and by limiting the number of people who have access to truly secret material to a minimum, much could be done to ease the burden on hard-pressed security services.

4. Potential sexpionage victims must be made much more aware of the real risks they run, mainly when visiting Soviet-bloc countries, but

also at home. If the need is there, the KGB mount effective entrapments in virtually any country in the world. The complexity of many operations and the range of technology available should be made clear.

So far as the victims and potential victims are concerned, they should treat the risk of entrapment far more seriously than many at present do. Without behaving in an offensively suspicious way towards Soviet and Sovet-bloc citizens in general, they should have no doubt that they might well be KGB agents. If they are compromised, they should report matters immediately to their embassy and never attempt to buy off the KGB with low-grade classified material. As explained, such a ploy is often used to switch the blackmail hold from sex material to pictures showing the victim performing a criminal act in handing over secrets.

Sexpionage, it is clear, is an effective, relatively inexpensive technique of espionage and subversion. But, despite its advantages, the West should be wary of adopting it. There is some evidence that both the British and the American intelligence services have carried out limited sexpionage operations, in Ulster and Latin America. But I could find nothing to suggest that wide and general use of the technique is now a part of routine information gathering.

Perhaps the kind of moral rectitude that made it unthinkable for Henry Stimson to condone the reading of private letters has been outdated by social change. Maybe we are all the poorer as a result. But ethical boundaries must still be drawn in intelligence gathering, as in every other sphere of human activity. During World War II an American statesman was asked if he thought the Allies would defeat fascism. "I am sure we will," he replied. "My only fear is that we shall have to become fascist ourselves to do so."

The risk that by taking the necessary measures to safeguard our interests we shall ultimately destroy the way of life being defended is a real one. When expediency becomes the sole justification for an intelligence operation and pragmatism is the only consideration for adopting a technique of subversion, we are taking dangerous steps along the road to internal moral collapse. Once the principle is accepted that society has the right, for whatever purpose, to invade the most intimate moments of a person's private life, to manipulate their emotions and destroy their dignity, we bestow on the security services that most dangerous of alliances—power without responsibility. That menacing combination, in the words of William Gladstone, has been the prerogative of the harlot throughout the ages.

Commentary on Sources

The obvious problem which confronts any writer researching material for an exposé of modern espionage techniques is the reliability of sources. People who have the information you need may not only have very good reasons for not talking under any circumstances, they often have even better reasons for telling you the exact opposite of the truth with the bland sincerity of a professional confidence trickster selling you the Empire State Building. In the latter case, it is at least possible to check, against documents of proven authenticity, the value of his apparently convincing claims. No such check is usually possible in the esoteric world of espionage. People may lie to you inadvertently, believing they speak the truth; they may lie out of bravado or to make themselves seem important; they may lie because it will pay them to do so; or because they wish to have erroneous information made public. No author in this minefield of potential fabrication can afford to ignore the extremely efficient disinformation services of intelligence organizations. Not only the big and powerful ones, but also every sort of pressure group and revolutionary movement from the IRA to the British Monday Club have ther own vested interest in helping you see the world through their eyes. The victims of sexpionage operations usually try to minimize their stupidity, the organizers the extent of their culpability. Like Alice in Wonderland the world of sexpionage in particular and espionage in general leaves one astonished, aghast, and only able to murmur, "curiouser and curiouser."

How then can one attempt to write an account which even approximates to the truth, an exposé based on fact rather than an imaginative commentary which goes drifting off like a hot-air balloon, with truth thrown overboard to give greater lift?

In researching this book I used three major types of sources: published material ranging from books to newspaper and magazine articles; formal interviews, usually given on a non-attributable basis; and informal conversations with a wide variety of people.

PUBLISHED SOURCES: These included all the major books and studies of modern espionage, a list of which will be found in the bibliography. Here the authenticity of the material must be a matter of judgment, although opinions expressed by authoritative reviewers, the nature of sources listed by a particular author, and careful cross-reference to similar works provide a useful guide. Even so, many published works must be regarded with suspicion because books are a primary weapon in the disinformation-purveyor's arsenal. A book which, like this one for example, attacks the subversion techniques of the KGB, could easily be based on material, factual or fanciful, provided by the CIA. This most certainly is not the case; but you do, of course, only have my word for it and were it otherwise I would be making exactly the same statement!

With the help of two research assistants, I have consulted more than 20,000 printed articles from the newspaper and magazine archives of six countries. Journalists, by the very speed and nature of their craft, frequently make mistakes. Comparing one story as published in eight or nine different publications across Europe, for example, one may find as many changes in a date, an address, a name, or a description. Such errors are irritating but do not necessarily detract from the overall picture provided. By making endless comparisons, by detailed cross-reference one can, eventually, draw together an image which is greater than the parts. Stories are subjected to security checks in all countries; in Britain editors have not only the ubiquitous Offical Secrets Act to contend with but also D-Notices, a system whereby the government "requests" the censorship of a particular item. Journalists by-and-large resent such intrusions and attempt to circumvent them. Anybody researching espionage must become adept at reading between the lines and making connections. Sometimes Homer nods and quite substantial secrets fall through the gaps in the system. It was through such lapses, for example, that the name of an early director of the Secret Intelligence Service was published and the location of the Security Service's London base first became known (unless, of course, one prefers to believe all such slips to be deliberate leaks for matters of deep but inexplicable policy). In this respect comparison between several editions of the same paper, where a major spy story is running, can be extremely valuable. Sudden cuts, the hammering of lines of type to make them illegible, or the dropping of a brief news item can all be significant. The British press has an often subtle device of running two stories, one highly dramatic, the other apparently innocuous, side-by-side when they want to draw an otherwise unmentionable connection.

These techniques should not be dismissed as the tricks of journalists. A recent estimate of the major sources of intelligence used by the great powers indicated that around eighty percent was drawn from "white material," that is, openly published, freely available articles and reports. Of the balance, some fifteen percent of information came from electronic espionage, and five percent from agents, defectors, casual informers, and similar sources. By feeding masses of white material into computers, quite a number of useful secrets can be gleaned. The journey of a particular government official to a certain place at a certain time. The expulsion of an embassy official following a seemingly unimportant raid or arrest. Of such, to a great extent, is the kingdom of espionage and of espionage exposé.

INTERVIEWS: As far as these were concerned, authenticity was a matter of judgment and character assessment. But, again, there were some obvious guidelines. Why was the information being given? At no time did I offer money or a more interesting bribe than a drink. The women I spoke to seemed genuine and their stories checked out, as far as checking was possible, with information from other sources. But it must be added that I reached them in the first place through contacts who might have a vested interest in spreading disinformation. I can only say that I believed them to be sincere, reliable, and honest, and nothing I have read or learned subsequently has caused me to alter my view.

In the text certain conversations are given as direct quotations, in order to give the reader a feeling for the event. In some cases these are based on notes I made during or after the interviews or took from tape recordings. These have been edited for the sake of brevity in one or two instances. Other, short, pieces of conversation are invented, since there is no way of knowing exactly what words were used. However, all such imaginary conversations are based on careful research and correspond as closely as possible to the actual remarks made.

INFORMAL CONVERSATIONS: These ranged from talks in pubs with contacts to discussions over lunch with men with security backgrounds. Once again, lies, through deliberate policy or inadvertence, cannot be ruled out. Where possible all the information given to me was crosschecked against material from different sources. A few of my informers were as anxious to have their views published as others were reluctant.

Information about the SIS brothels in Belfast, for example, came from a number of sources. None of them is entirely hostile to the aims of the IRA. The British authorities have denied their version of these events.

Books on espionage can be written by two kinds of people. One type has worked inside the system and then come out of it, either through retirement or resignation. This type has his own axe to grind: the person who retired to praise the object of his labors, the person who resigned to tear down the fabric which now offends him. The second kind of writer is the outsider, the investigator with no official or unofficial links to the intelligence services. Such an author may be motivated by interest in the subject, a feeling that the public should know what is being done against them or in their name by the faceless, nameless men in espionage; or he might be motivated by simple greed, a desire to cash in on a subject of wide public interest. The published work is witness for both the defense and the prosecution; it must be left to the reader to decide its reliability and that of its author.

Bibliography

The following newspapers and magazines were studied from over a period stretching back some twenty-five years: (Dublin) *Hibernia, Sunday Sun;* (Frankfurt) *Frankfurter Zeitung;* (Hamburg) *Stern, Die Welt; Quick, Neue Revue,* (London) *Daily Express, Daily Mail, Daily Mirror, Daily Sketch, Daily Telegraph, The Guardian, The Observer, Sunday Telegraph, Sunday Times, Times;* (Milan) *Oggi;* (New York) *Newsweek, Time;* (Offenburg, W Germany) *Bunte Oesterreich Illustrierte;* (Paris) *L'Express, Le Figaro, France-Soir, L'Humanité, Le Monde, Paris-Match*

GENERAL WORKS

Barron, John. *KGB: The Secret Work of the Soviet Secret Agents* (New York, 1974)

Boycard, Robert. *The Secret Services of Europe.* Translated by R. Leslie-Melville (London, 1960)

Crawford, Iain. *The Profumo Affair: A Crisis in Contemporary Society* (London, 1963)

Deacon, Richard. *A History of the Russian Secret Service* (New York, 1972)

Dulles, Allen. *The Craft of Intelligence* (New York, 1963)

Gramont, Sanche de. *The Secret War: The Story of International Espionage Since World War II* (New York, 1962)

Greig, Ian. *The Assault on the West* (New York, 1974)

Guevara, Che. *The Complete Bolivian Diaries of Che Guevara and Other Captured Documents.* Daniel James, ed. (Briarcliff Manor, N.Y., 1968)

Hagen, Louis. *The Secret War for Europe: A Dossier of Espionage* (London, 1968)

Hamilton, Peter. *Espionage and Subversion in an Industrial Society: An Examination and Philosophy of Defense for Management* (Atlantic Highlands, N.J., 1967)

Hoehne, Heinz, and Solling, Hermann. *Network: The Truth About General Gehlen and His Network* (London, 1967)

Hutton, J. Bernard. *Struggle in the Dark: How Russian and Other Iron Curtain Spies Operate* (London, 1969)

BIBLIOGRAPHY

Ind, Allison. *A History of Modern Espionage* (London, 1965)

Irving, Clive, and Hall, Ron, and Wallington, Jeremy *Scandal '63 A Study of the Profumo Affair* (London, 1963)

Kahn, David. *The Codebreakers* (New York, 1973)

MacKenzie, Compton. *Water on the Brain* (London, 1953)

Marchetti, Victor, and Marks, John D *The C.I.A and the Cult of Intelligence* (New York, 1974)

Newman, Richard. *Spy and Counter-Spy: The Story of the British Secret Service* (London, 1970)

Page, Bruce, and Knightly, Philip, and Leitch, David. *Philby: The Spy Who Betrayed a Generation* (London, 1968)

Perrault, Gilles. *L'Erreur* (Paris, 1971)

Ransom, Harry H. *Intelligence Establishment* (Cambridge, Mass., 1970)

Richings, M. G. *Espionage: The Story of the Secret Service of the English Crown* (London, 1934)

Romanov, A. I *Nights Are Longest There: A Memoir of the Soviet Security Services*. Translated by Gerald Brooke (Boston, 1972)

Ross, Thomas, and Wise, David. *The Espionage Establishment* (New York, 1968)

Rowan, Richard Wilmer, and Deindorfer, R. G. *Secret Service: Thirty-Three Centuries of Espionage* (London, 1969)

Seale, P., and McConville, M. *Philby: The Long Road to Moscow* (New York, 1974)

Seth, Ronald. *Encyclopedia of Espionage: From the Age of Jericho to the Age of James Bond* (New York, 1974)

Smith, R. Harris. *OSS. The Secret History of America's First Central Intelligence Agency* (Berkeley, Calif , 1972)

Taylor, John W., and Monday, David. *Spies in the Sky* (New York, 1973)

Tully, Andrew. *Super Spies* (New York, 1970)

White, John Baker. *The Soviet Spy System* (London, 1948)

Williams, David. *Not in the Public Interest: The Problem of Security in a Democracy* (London, 1965)

BIOGRAPHY

Baden-Powell, Robert. *Adventures of a Spy* (London, 1936)

Baillie-Stewart, Norman. *The Officer in the Tower* (London, 1967)

Bernikow, Louise. *Abel* (New York, 1970)

Bulloch, John. *MI-5: The Origin and History of the British Counter-Espionage Service* (London, 1963)

BIBLIOGRAPHY

Charlton, Warwick. *Stephen Ward Speaks* (London, 1963)
Courtney, Anthony. *Sailor in a Russian Frame* (London, 1968)
Gehlen, Reinhard. *The Service* (New York, 1972)
Kersten, Felix. *The Kersten Memoirs, 1940-1945* (London, 1956)
Levy, Norma. *I, Norma Levy* (London, 1973)
Lonsdale, Gordon. *Spy: Twenty Years in Soviet Secret Service* (New York, 1965)
Lucas, Norman. *Spycatcher: A Biography of Detective-Superintendent George Gordon Smith* (London, 1973)
Philby, Kim. *My Silent War* (New York, 1972)
Sillitoe, Percy. *Cloak Without Dagger* (London, 1957)
Strong, Kenneth. *Intelligence at the Top: The Recollections of an Intelligence Officer* (New York, 1969)
Vassall, John. *Vassall: The Autobiography of a Spy* (London, 1975)
Wynne, Greville. *The Man From Moscow: The Story of Wynne and Penkovsky* (London, 1967)

SPIES AND DEFECTORS

Bulloch, John, and Miller, Henry. *Spy Ring: The Full Story of the Naval Secrets Case* (London, 1961)
Cookridge, Edward Henry. *Shadow of a Spy: The Complete Dossier on George Blake* (London, 1967)
Houghton, Harry. *Operation Portland: The Autobiography of a Spy* (London, 1972)
Her Majesty's Stationery Office (HMSO). *Security Procedures on the Public Service*. April 5, 1962
HMSO. *Interim report by the Committee of Enquiry into the Vassall Case*. November 1962
HMSO. *Report of Tribunal Appointed to Inquire into the Vassall Case and Related Matters*. Chairman, Lord Radcliffe. April 1963
HMSO. *Tribunal Appointed to Inquire into the Vassall Case and Related Matters—Minutes of Evidence*. June 1963
HMSO. *Lord Denning's Report* (Profumo). September 1963
HMSO. *Prime Minister's Standing Security Commission Report*. June 1965
HMSO. *Board of Inquiry Report of Security Commission on the Bossard and Allen Case*. September 1965
Kirkpatrick, L. B., Jr. *Spy with the Old School Tie: Philby* (London 1969)
Mather, John S., and Seaman, Donald. *The Great Spy Scandal* (London, 1955)
West, Rebecca. *Vassall Affair* (London, 1963)

BIBLIOGRAPHY

D-NOTICES AND OFFICIAL SECRETS ACT

Aitken, Jonathan. *Officially Secret* (London, 1971)

Hedkley, Peter, and Aynsley, Cyril. *The D-Notice Affair* (London, 1968)

HMSO. *Report of the Committee of Privy Counsellors Appointed to Inquire into D-Notice Matters.* June 1967

HMSO. *The D-Notice System.* 1967

Pincher, Chapman. "Press Freedom and National Security," *Journalism Today,* Vol. I. No. 2., 1968

ROLE OF INTELLIGENCE

Benjamin, Roger W., and Edinger, Lewis J. *Conditions for Military Control over Foreign Policy Decisions in Major States: An Historical Explanation* (Ann Arbor, 1971)

Cooper, Chester L. "The CIA and Decision Making," *Foreign Affairs,* January, 1972, pp. 223-36.

Glickman, Harvey, and Wilson, Harold. *The Problem of Internal Security in Great Britain 1948–53* (New York, 1954)

UNPUBLISHED AND RESTRICTED PUBLICATION DOCUMENTS

Committee for the Limitation of Secret Police Powers Original Statement June 1956. Second Statement 1957

Committee of 100, Hampstead Group. *Mail Interception and Telephone Tapping*

KGB-prepared smear documents circulated to British press regarding Anthony Courtney

MI-5/Foreign Office. *Their Trade Is Treachery.* 1964

MILITARY

Elliott-Batemen, Michael, ed. *The Fourth Dimension of Warfare,* Vol. I, *Intelligence, Subversion, and Resistance* (New York, 1970)

NATO. *The North Atlantic Treaty Organization* (Brussels)

NATO. Unclassified documents relating to establishment of SHAPE (Brussels)

Pretty, R.T., and Archer, D.H.R. *Jane's Weapon Systems* (London, 1970)

Royal United Services Institute (RUSI) and Brassey's Defense Yearbooks

RUSI. *British Arms and Strategy 1970–1980* (1969 pamphlet)

Strong, Kenneth. *Men of Intelligence: A Study of the Roles and Decisions of Chiefs of Intelligence from World War I to the Present Day* (New York, 1972)

Index

Abel, Col. Rudolf Ivanovich, 30, 37, 59
Aden Gang, 123
Aerial espionage, 115
Air-to-air missiles, *see* Missiles
Alexander II (Czar of Russia), 24
Amnesty for sexpionage victims, 70–71, 152
Anderson, Jack, 21
Andropov, Yuri Vladimirovich, 27–29, 82
"Archers, The" (British television program), 38
Assassinations, euphemisms for, 30n; *see also* Executions
Astor, Lord William W., 132
Atomic devices, China explodes (1965), 6
Atomic Energy Commission (AEC; U.S.), 6
Australian Labour party, 130
Avdayev, Col. A. I., 43

Baden-Powell, Sir Robert, 4
Baetge, Gertie, 97
Barron, John, 23
Bauer, Laura Gutierrez (Haydee Tamara Bunke; Laura Martínez; code name: Tania), 61–65
Behavior modification drugs, 148–49
Beria, Lavrenti Pavlovich, 26–27, 66
BfV, *see* Bundesamt für Verfassungsschutz
Bider, Nadja, 61
Big Bird (U.S. satellite), 6
Big Paddy (code name), 125

Black Chamber (cryptologic section of U.S. military intelligence), 5
Blacks, defined, 34
Blue movies, 100
BND, *see* Bundesnachrichtendienst
Board of Trade (British), 19, 135
Boehm, Gerhard, 112
Bolivian Communist party, 63, 64
Bolshevik Revolution (1917), 24, 43
Bossard, Frank, 31
Brandt, Werner, 84
Brandt, Willy, 153
Breast transmitters, 6, 142
Brezhnev, Leonid, 27, 28
British Army Intelligence, 123
   in World War II, 126–28
British Army units
   Royal Army Medical Corps, 131
   1st Battalion of Royal Highland Fusiliers, 124
British Communist party, 113
British Conservative party, 75
British counterintelligence, *see* Security Service
British intelligence, *see* Secret Intelligence Service
British Labour party, 74
British press, 156–57
Brockerhoff, Maria, 97
Brooks, Gerald, 59
Brothels
   British use of, 122–28, 135–36
   in France, 126–28
   in Northern Ireland, 20, 122–26, 128, 157

163

INDEX

Brothels (*cont.*)
  Nazi, 3, 98
  See also Call girls; Pension Clausewitz; Prostitutes; Ravens; Swallows
Buckingham, 2nd Duke of (George Villiers), 132
Buechner, Elfriede, 86
Bundesamt für Verfassungsschutz (BfV; Federal Office for the Protection of the Constitution; West German), 92
  arrests made by
    Dreesen, 100
    Helfmann, 86
  Helmcke in employ of, 95, 96
  KGB aware of every operation of (1960s), 76
  Luedke and, 105, 110
  spinsters viewed as security risks by, 78
Bundesnachrichtendienst (BND; Federal Intelligence Service; West German), 92
  attack on Schwirkman and, 139
  founder of, 111
  Luedke and, 109
    involved in Luedke's death, 111
    KGB plans to deliver Luedke to, 109
  Senj and, 106–7
Bunke, Erich, 61
Bunke, Haydee Tamara (Laura Martínez; Laura Gutierrez Bauer; code name: Tania), 61–65
Bureau of State Security (South African), 5
Burgess, Guy, 114

California, University of, at San Diego, 148
Call girls, British, 135–37
Cameras
  film, 144–45
  single-lens reflex, 144
  still, 143–45
    problems presented by, 143–44
    used with vaginal transmitters, 145–46
  television, 146
  See also Photographic equipment
Camp David (CIA training center), 34–35
Camus, Capt. André, 88
Card index system
  Beria expands, 26–27
  maintained by Okhrana, 24
Castro, Fidel, 21, 62, 64
Central Intelligence Agency (CIA), 7
  in alleged plot against Indonesia, 18
  Bolivian counterinsurgency forces trained by, 64
  Czech refugees turning over information to (1968), 106
  defensive sexpionage operations of, 21
  euphemisms used by, 30*n*
  KGB training manual obtained by, 42
  KGB relationship with, 5
  and Luedke's death, 105, 111
  main European training center of, 34–35
  K. Martin uncovered by, 99
  miniature television cameras used by, 146
  Penkovsky contacts, 130
  as prime target of KGB, 43
  and Rousseau case, 88
  SIS and
    SIS compared with, 129
    SIS relationship with, 5
  and technical advances in electronic equipment, 140–42
  on trail of A.M. Rinaldi, 115
  warned about Vassall, 90
Cheka (Chrezvychainaya Komissiya po Borbe s Kontrrevolutsiei i Sabotazham; Extraordinary Commission for Combating

164

INDEX

Counterrevolution and Sabotage; Soviet Union), 25–26
Chesterfield, 4th Earl of (Philip Dormer Stanhope), 9
China (People's Republic of China), explodes nuclear device (1965), 6
Chrezvychainaya Komissiya po Borbe s Kontrrevolutsiei i Sabotazham (Cheka; Extraordinary Commission for Combating Counterrevolution and Sabotage; Soviet Union), 25–26
Chip circuits, 6
described, 140
Churchill, Sir Winston, 126–27, 131
CIA, *see* Central Intelligence Agency
Ciano, Count Galeazzo, 98
Clean work, defined, 40
Cohen, Lona, 30, 75
Cohen, Morris, 30, 75
Cold War, 5, 114
Combat training of swallows and ravens, 40
COMLINT (communications intelligence; U.S. satellite), 5
Commerce Ministry (East German), 84
Communications intelligence (COMLINT; U.S. satellite), 5
Communist Youth League (Komsomol, Soviet), 27, 48
Confidential (NATO secrecy classification), 104
"Coronation Street" (TV show), 38
Cosmic Top Secret (NATO secrecy classification), 104
Council of Ministers (Politburo; Soviet), 29
Counterinsurgency forces in Bolivia, 63–64
Courtney, Commander Anthony, 70–75
Courtney, Elizabeth, 73–74
Cuban missile crisis (1962), 130
Cuban Women's Militia, 62
Czech Central Committee, 39
Czech foreign intelligence service (Statni Tajna Bezpcnost; STB), 18

Czechoslovakia, intervention in (1968), 106

DDR (Deutsche Demokratische Republik; East Germany), intelligence of, *see* Ministerium für Staatsicherheit
Deacon, Richard, 24, 26
Dead drops, defined, 79
Deaths of prostitutes in Northern Ireland, 125, 126; *see also* Assassinations; Executions; Suicides
Debray, Regis, 64
Defections
attempts to have Ivanov defect, 133, 134
of Demidov, 40
helping to discover activities of subverted officials, 17
of Krotkov, 66, 70
of Lyalin, 134–35
of Philby, 114
of Y. Runge, 79–82
of Sorokin, 37
of Vera, 46, 58
Defense Department (U.S.), as prime target of KGB, 43
Defense Ministry (Italian), 115
Defense plans
of NATO
changed following Luedke affair, 112
Suetterlins obtain, 79, 80
West German, H. Suetterlin obtains, 80
De Gaulle, Charles, 66, 68, 116
Dejean, Marie Claire, 66–67
Dejean, Maurice, 65–70
Del (code name), 43–44
Demidov, Sasha, 40–41
Diplomatic immunity
as issue, 72, 74–75
of Lyalin, 135
of E. Rousseau, 86
Direction Générale des Etudes et Recherches, 86

165

INDEX

Dirty tricks, defined, 5
Dirty work, defined, 40–41
Dolly Fosset (IRA operation; Operation Leo), 126
Dreesen, Rolf, 100
Drugs, 148–49
Dubcek, Alexander, 106
Dubenskaya, I. B., 43
Dulles, Allen, 23
Dzerzhinsky, Feliks Edmundovich, 25, 28

East German intelligence, *see* Ministerium für Staatssicherheit
Eastman Kodak Co., 142
Edinburgh, Duke of (Philip of Mountbatten), 82
Education, *see* Training
El-Djeih (Algerian magazine), 141
Electronic equipment
   in Dejean entrapment, 68
   in embassies, 81, 138
   in Guibaud entrapment, 69–70
   in hotel room occupied by Queen Elizabeth II, 82
   how to install, 31
   in Latour entrapment, 16
   K. Martin uses, 99
   in massage parlors, 34
   in NATO infiltration, 115
   in Pension Clausewitz, 93, 96
   in Salon Kitty, 98
   technological developments in (1960s and 1970s), 6–7, 139–42, 145–46, 148
Electronic pills, 141–42
ELINT (electronic intelligence-gathering), 5–6
Elizabeth I (Queen of England), 4
Elizabeth II (Queen of England), 82
Embassies, infiltrated, 81, 138
England, *see entries beginning with word* British
Entrapment, description of typical, 147–48

Executions
   attempts on Schwirkman's life, 139
   of Bossman Jim, 126
   euphemisms for, 30*n*
   of Heidel, 59
   of Helmcke, 92, 97–98
   of Kirsch, 94
   of Luedke, 105, 109–11
   of O. and M. Morales, 60
   of Penkovsky, 30*n*
   of Stewart, 126

Fallax (NATO exercise), 76
Fallax 66 (NATO exercise), 76
Federal Bureau of Investigation (FBI), 87
   as prime target of KGB, 43
   Security Service compared with, 129
Federal Republic of Germany, *see* West Germany; *and specific West German intelligence agencies*
Female prostitutes, *see* Brothels; Call girls; Prostitutes; Swallows
Film cameras, characteristics of, 144–45
Films
   blue, 100
   British, shown in training, 38
   Pension Clausewitz in, 97
   sex-education, 51
   ultra-high speed, 142
First Chief Directorate (KGB), 28–31
First World War (1914–1918), 4
V, Department, 30
Foreign Office (British), 136, 150
Foreign Office (West German), 85
Foreign Trade, Ministry of (Soviet), 73
"Forsythe Saga, The" (TV show), 38
Four Square Laundry (Security Service information-gathering operation), IRA attacks on, 125–26
French counterintelligence, *see* Service de Documentation Extérieure et de Contre-Espionnage
French millitary intelligence, 128
From Russia with Love (Fleming), 14

166

INDEX

Gaczyna (spy school; Soviet), 37–39
Galbraith, Thomas, 90
Gast, Willi Kunt (Yevgeni Yevgenevich Runge), 77–82, 153
Gehlen, Reinhard, 111
Gelhaar, Emma, 94
German Democratic Republic (DDR; East Germany), *see* Ministerium für Staatssicherheit
German High Command (World War II), 7
Germany
 East, *see* Ministerium für Staatssicherheit
 Nazi, sexpionage in, 93, 98
 West, number of spies in (1966), 115; *see also* Bundesamt für Verfassungsschutz; Bundesnachrichtendienst; Militarischer Abschirmdienst
Getty, J. Paul, 131
Gladstone, Sir William, 154
Glavnoye Razvedyvatelnoye Upravleniye (GRU; Soviet military intelligence), 30, 130, 131, 134
Goebbels, Joseph P., 93
Gottfried, Harald, 112
Grapentin, Edeltraud, 111–12
Grays, defined, 34
Great Britain, *see* entries beginning with word British
Gribanov, Gen. Oleg, 69
Grimm, Col. Johannes, 112
GRU (Glavnoye Razvedyvatelnoye Upravleniye; Soviet military intelligence), 30, 130, 131, 134
Guerrilla war in Bolivia, 63–64
Guevara, Che (code name: Ramon), 61–65
Guibaud, Col. Louis, 69
Guided missiles, *see* Missiles
Guillaume, Guenter, 153

Hawk missile guidance system, parts of, stolen, 108–9

Health studios in Northern Ireland, 112, 124, 126
Hearst, Patty, 65*n*
Heidel, Gudrun, 58–60
Heinz, Leonore (Leonore Suetterlin; code name: Lola), 76–83
Helfmann, Karl (Red Casanova), 83–86, 96
Helke, Trude, 101–2
Helmcke, Hans Albert Heinrich
 career of, 93–96
 characteristics of, 92–93
 death of, 92, 97–98
Hempel, Ingeborg, 96
Heydrich, Gen. Reinhard, 98
Hill, Capt. George, 30*n*
Himmler, Heinrich, 98
Hitler, Adolf, 128
Hollis, Sir Roger Henry, 129–31, 133, 134
Holzer, Franz, 97
Home, Sir Alec Douglas, 75
Home Office (British), 129
Homosexual ravens
 most publicized entrapment by, 89–91
 training of, 56–57
 uses of, 36
Homosexuals
 brothels catering to, 98
 vulnerability of, 153
Hospitality fund of British Foreign Office, 136
Houghton, Harry, 130
Hutton, Bernard, 39

Illegals, defined, 30
Imprisonment
 of M. and L. Cohen, 75
 of Helfmann, 86
 of Helmcke, 96
 of Ramminger, 120
 of E. Rousseau, 88
 of H. and L. Suetterlin, 82–83
 of Vassall, 90
Imre, Nihat, 106, 116

167

INDEX

Index system, see Card index system
Indig, Josy, 95, 96
Indoctrination, political, 36, 39, 49, 50
Indonesia, coup in (1965), 18
Industrial espionage, 73
   Directorate T's role in, 30
   Helfmann involved in, 84-85
Industrial Security Directorate (KGB), 31
Inertial navigation platform, theft of, 119
Informers, Okhrana, 24
Intelligence gathering
   electronic, 5-6
   as secondary activity, 151
Internal Affairs, Ministry of (NKVD; Soviet), 27
Internal Security (report), 115
Intourist (Soviet tourist organization), 11, 12, 72, 139
Irish Republican Army (IRA), 155, 158
   attack mounted by, 125-26
   faulty intelligence on, 122-23
Italian counterintelligence, 115
Ivan the Terrible (Czar of Russia), 24
Ivanov, Eugene (Fox Face), 131-34

Jellicoe, 1st Earl (John Rushworth), 136

Kapustin Yar (Soviet air base), 5
Karlin, George (Yuri Vasilevich Krotkov), 65-70
Karlsruhe Atomic Center (West German), 112
Keeler, Christine, 72, 131-34, 152
Kersten, Felix, 98
KGB, see Komitet Gosudarstvennoy Bezopasnosti
Khovanskaya, Lydia, 67-68
Khrushchev, Nikita, 48, 51
Kidnappings
   of Baetge, 97
   of Helmcke, 97
Kieling, Wolfgang, 97
Kipling, Rudyard, 112
Kirsch, Heinrich, 94

Knoppe, Wolf Diethard, 118-21
Komitet Gosudarstvennoy Bezopasnosti (KGB; Committee of State Security; Soviet), 23-32
   building housing, 28-29
   estimated number of agents of, in Europe and U.S., 70
   historical background of, 24-27
   organization and control of, 29-31
   prime targets of, 43
   size of, 50
   staff and power of, 23-24
Komsomol (Communist Youth League; Soviet), 27, 48
Krivitsky, Gen. Walter, 26
Krogers (Lona and Morris Cohen), 30, 75
Krokodil (Soviet magazine), 19-20
Kronberg, Sobolevskaya Larissa, 68
Krotkov, Yuri Vasilevich (George Karlin), 65-70
Kunavin, Col. Leonid Petrovich, 66, 68
Kuzazova, Lydia, 33-35

Labyav, Dimitri, 56
Lambton, Lord, 136, 152
Laser beams, 6, 148
Latour, Philippe, 10-17, 32
Le Carré, John, 78
Legaev, Vladimir, 24
Legals, defined, 72
Lemnitzer, Gen. Lyman L., 104
Lenin, Vladimir I., 25, 50
Lenin Technical High School, 40
Lenses, light-intensification, 146-47; *see also* Photographic equipment
Leo (IRA operation; Dolly Fosset operation), 126
L'Erreur (The Error; Perrault), 88
Levy, Norma (Norma Russell), 136
Lindgren, Maj. Per, 37
Linowsky, Helena, 117
Linowsky, Josef, 117-21
Lipton, Marcus, 137
Litton LM III navigation boxes, theft of, 118-19

168

INDEX

Lolite (instrument), 147
Lonsdale, Gordon (Konon Trofimovich Molody), 37, 59
Lorenz, Marie, 21
Luedke, Adm. Hermann (Sonny Boy), 102
   becomes KGB spy, 107-9, 111, 115, 116
   execution of, 105, 109-11
   framed, 105-7, 109
   post held by, 103-4
Lyalin, Oleg, 134-35

Mafia, 91
Maiziere, Gen. Ulrich de, 102
Male prostitutes, *see* Homosexual ravens; Ravens
Maleter, Gen. Pál, 27
Mandell, Arnold, 148
Marggraf, Martin, 81-82
Martin, Karl, 98-99
Martin, Ludwig, 105
Martínez, Antonio, 63
Martínez, Laura (Haydee Tamara Bunke; Laura Gutierrez Bauer; code name: Tania), 61-65
Marx-Engels School, 36, 39
Mary (Queen of Scots), 4
Massage parlors, 34
Medical examinations
   of Foreign Office call girls, 136
   of prospective swallows, 48-49
Menzhinsky, Vyacheslav, 25
MfS, *see* Ministerium für Staatssicherheit
MGB (Ministry of State Security; Soviet), 27
MI-5 (British wartime counterintelligence), 19, 128; *see also* Security Service
MI-6 (British wartime intelligence), 128; *see also* Secret Intelligence Service
Middle-aged women as ravens' targets, 56
Middle East War (1973), 5
Militärischer Abschirmdienst (West German military counterintelligence), 102-3, 105
Mind-altering drugs, 148-49
Ministerium für Staatssicherheit (MfS; East German Ministry of State Security), 153
   agents of
      Helfmann, 83-85
      Helmcke, 95, 96
      K. Martin, 98-99
      L. Martínez, 61-62
   blue movies used by, 100
   obtains atomic secrets, 112
   overextensive classification by, 153
Missile centers, NATO
   aerial photographing of, 115
   Suetterlin discovers locations of, 80
Missiles
   Hawk missile guidance systems, Luedke steals parts of, 108-9
   homing heads of, Latour reveals information on, 15-16
   Penkovsky and NATO missile capability, 130
   theft of Sidewinder, 117, 119-20
Mitrofanova, T. V., 43
Molody, Konon Trofimovich (Gordon Lonsdale), 37, 59
Monday Club (British), 155
Morales, Miriam, 60
Morales, Otto, 60
Moral Essays (Pope), 132
Movies, *see* Films
Muñoz, Gonzálo López, 63
Murders, *see* Executions

National Security Council (U.S.), as prime KGB target, 43
NATO, *see* North Atlantic Treaty Organization
Naval Intelligence Division (British), 90
News of the World (British newspaper), 71
New York Press Agency, 95
Nikon (still camera), problems presented by, 143-44

INDEX

Nixon, Richard M., 21
NKVD (Ministry of Internal Affairs; Soviet), 27
North Atlantic Treaty Organization (NATO), 76
   founded (1949), 114–15
   infiltration of, 9, 20, 101–21
      by H. and L. Suetterlin, 76–80
   Penkovsky and missile capability of, 130
Northern Ireland, British operations in, 20, 122–26, 128, 157
Nuclear devices, China explodes (1965), 6

Official Secrets Act (British), 124, 156
Okhrana (Department of State Protection; Czarist Russia), 24
Optical fibers, uses of, 144

Penkovsky, Col. Oleg, 7, 30*n*, 130
Pension Clausewitz (West Berlin), 93–97
   as high-class brothel, 94–95
   life at, 96
   film about, 97
   as nerve center of spy ring, 93, 96
Perrault, Gilles, 88
Petrov, Vladimir, 130
Petrovich, Dimitri, 73, 74
Phantom (jet plane), plans for theft of, 119, 121
Philby, Kim (Harold Adrian Russell Philby), 73, 113–16
Philip V (King of Spain), 4
Photographic equipment, 142–48
   installation of, 31–32
   technological developments in, 146–48
   uses of
      in call-girl network, 136
      in Dejean entrapment, 68
      in Guibaud entrapment, 70
      in industrial espionage, 85
      in Latour entrapment, 14–16
      in Lyalin entrapment, 135
      by K. Martin, 99
      in massage parlors, 34
      in Northern Ireland brothels, 123, 124
      to photograph documents, 79–81, 85
      in Rohrer case, 35
      by second Chief Directorate, 31–32
      in training schools, 50, 54–55
Photographic reconnaissance satellites, 6
Physical education in training of swallows and ravens, 40
Physical requirements for ravens and swallows, 35
Pieschel, Leopold, 81, 82
Pilkington Perkin-Elmer (British firm), 147
Plesetsk (Soviet air base), 5
Polish intelligence service, 117
Politburo (Council of Ministers; Soviet), 29
Political indoctrination, 36, 39, 49, 50
Pompidou, Georges, 88
Pope, Alexander, 132
Powers, Gary, 28, 59
Prakhovka (spy school), 37
Press, British, 156–57
Prison terms, *see* Imprisonment
Profumo, John, 71, 132–34, 152
Profumo Affair, 96, 129, 131–34
Prostitutes, Ward as provider of, 131; *see also* Brothels; Call girls; Ravens; Swallows
Psychological aspects of attraction to sexpionage, 20–21
Purges, Soviet (1930s), 25–26

Radio Corporation of America (RCA), 146
Radio-microphones, miniaturization of, 140–41; *see also* Electronic equipment

170

INDEX

Radio teeth, 6, 142
Radio transmitters, miniaturization of, 141–42; *see also* Electronic equipment
Ramminger, Manfred, 117–21
Rank Precision Instruments (British firm), 146
Ravens
  selection requirements of, 36
  social background of, 44
  training of, 31, 40–42
    sexual, 41, 56
  See also Homosexual ravens
RCA (Radio Corporation of America), 146
Reconnaissance satellites, 6
Rice-Davies, Mandy, 131
Rinaldi, Angela Maria (Red Tsarina), 115
Rinaldi, Giorgio, 115
Riots in Northern Ireland (1970), 122, 123
Roemer, Irmgard, 85–86
Rohl, Barbel, 97
Rohl, Uwe, 97
Rohrer, Glen, 34–35
Rommel, Gen. Erwin, 126–28
Rousseau, Eugène, 86–88
Rousseau, Monique, 86–88
Royal Ulster Constabulary, Special Branch of, 122, 123, 129
Runge, Andrei, 81, 82
Runge, Valentina (Valentina Rusch), 81, 82
Runge, Yevgeni Yevgenevich (Willi Kunt Gast), 78–82, 153
Rusch, Valentina (Valentina Runge), 81, 82
Russell, Norma (Norma Levy), 136
Rutowski, Heinz, 102

S, Directorate (illegals directorate; KGB), 30
Salakov, Tania, 12–14, 32
Salon Kitty, 98
SAMOS series (U.S. satellites), 6
Satellites (space), 5, 6
Schellenberg, Walter, 98
Schenk, Hans Heinrich, 112
Schmidt, Kitty, 98
Schroeder, Gerhard, 80
Schwirkman, Horst, 138–39
Scotland Yard, 122
SDECE, *see* Service de Documentation Extérieure et de Contre-Espionnage
Second Chief Directorate (KGB), 31
Second World War (1939–1945), 7, 126–28
Secrecy grades, NATO's, 104
Secret classifications, need to reduce, 153
Secret Intelligence Service (SIS; British), 20, 153, 156, 158
  CIA relationship with, 5
  Czech refugees turning over information to (1968), 106
  euphemisms used by, 30*n*
  Luedke's death and, 105
  Penkovsky contacts, 130
  Philby in employ of, 114
  post-World War II activities of, 128
  rivalry between Security Service and, 129, 130
Secret (NATO security classification), 104
Secrets
  atomic, 112
  safeguarding, 150–54
  supplied by Helfmann, 85
  supplied by Luedke, 101–5, 107–9
  supplied by the Suetterlins, 80, 82
  supplied by Vassall, 90
  See also Defense plans; Missile centers; Missiles; Thefts
Security Service (British), 75, 156
  call-girl network of, 136–51
  diplomatic immunity issue and, 74
  Lyalin's defection and, 134–35
  operations of, in Northern Ireland, 20, 122–26, 128

INDEX

Security Service (British) (*cont.*)
   Profumo Affair and, 129, 131–34
   reactions of, to KGB sex traps, 18–19
   rivalry between SIS and, 129, 130
   and Vassall case, 91
Senj, Gen. Jan, 106, 111, 116
Serov, Gen. Ivan, 27
Service de Documentation Extérieure et de Contre-Espionage (SDECE), 16, 86–88
   Dejean entrapment and, 65–66
   Luedke's death and, 105
Sex education, 51–56
Sex schools, *see* Training
Sexual behavior, need for changed attitudes toward, to neutralize sexpionage, 151–52
SHAPE, *see* Supreme Headquarters Allied Powers Europe
Shooting practice at Lenin Technical High School, 41
Sidewinder AIM 9E (missile), theft of, 117, 119–20
Signal Research and Development Establishment (British), 146
Single-lens reflex cameras used in conjunction with optical fibers, 144
SIS, *see* Secret Intelligence Service
VI, Department (counterespionage service of the SS; German), 98
Smear campaigns, 9
   against Courtney, 71–75
Smithson, Tommy (Scarface), 123, 126
Socialist Revolutionary party (Soviet), 25
Sonar detection methods, Vassall passes information on, 90
Sorokin, Anatoli, 37, 44
South African Bureau of State Security, 5
Soviet Central Committee, 27, 29
Soviet Foreign Intelligence Residency, 43
Soviet intelligence, *see* Komitet Gosudarstvennoy Bezopasnosti
Soviet military intelligence (GRU; Glavnoye Razvedyvatelnoye Upravleniye), 30, 130, 131, 134
Spanish Civil War (1936–1939), 114
Special Air Services (British), 129
Special Branch of Royal Ulster Constabulary (Northern Ireland), 122, 123, 129
Spy satellites used in 1973 Middle East War, 5
Spy swaps, 75
   Abel–Powers, 59
   Brooks–Lonsdale, 59
   Courtney smear campaign and, 75
   Ramminger as useful in, 121
SS (Schutzstaffel) counterespionage service (Department VI; German), 98
Stalin, Joseph (Joseph Dzhugashvili), 24–28
Stange, Jurgen, 59
State Department (U.S.), as prime target of KGB, 43
State Protection, Department of (Okhrana; Czarist Russia), 24
State Security, Ministry of (MGB; Soviet), 27
Statni Tajna Bezpcnost (STB; Czech foreign intelligence), 18
Stewart, Sapper Ted, 126
Still cameras, 143–45
   problems presented by, 143–44
   used with vaginal transmitters, 145–46
Stimson, Henry, 4–5, 154
Stülpnagel, Gen. Heinrich von, 128
Submarine warfare secrets, Vassall obtains, 90
Subolov, Major, 17
Suetterlin, Heinz, 31, 76–83
Suetterlin, Leonore (Leonore Heinz; code name: Lola), 76–83
Suicides
   Boehm, 112
   Grapentin, 112
   Grimm, 112
   Guibaud, 70
   Schenk, 112

INDEX

L. Suetterlin, 76, 82–83
in training schools, 56
Ward, 134
H. Wendland, 110, 111
Sukarno, Achmed, 17–18
Supreme Headquarters Allied Powers Europe (SHAPE), 102–5, 109, 112
 moves to Belgium, 103, 108 116
Swallows (KGB prostitutes)
 social background of, 44
 training of, 31, 33–45, 49–57
  cost, 47
  at Gaczyna, 37–39
  KGB interrogations as part of, 41–42
  length and characteristics of, 36–37
  at Lenin Technical High School, 40–41
  manuals used in, 42–44
  physical education in, 40
  political indoctrination as part of, 36, 39, 49, 50
  selection requirements for, 35–36
  sex education in, 51–56
  at Verkhonoye, 33, 35, 46, 50, 58, 59
Swedish General Staff, 37

T. Directorate (KGB), 30, 134
Tape recorders, miniaturization of, 140; *see also* Electronic equipment
Taylor, Elizabeth, 131
Technological developments in electronic and photographic equipment, 6–7, 139–48
Television cameras, miniaturization of, 146; *see also* Photographic equipment
Teplyakova, Irina, 135
Thefts
 of inertial navigation platform, 119
 of Litton LM III navigation boxes, 118–19
 of parts of Hawk missile guidance system, 108–9
 of Sidewinder, 117, 119–20
Their Trade Is Treachery (British pamphlet), 19
Three-stage cascade system, described, 146
Tilney, John, 71
Torres, Gen. Juan José, 64
Training, *see* Swallows
Trial of the Twenty-One (1938), 26
Trotsky, Leon, 30n
Tyuratam (Soviet air base), 5

Ultra-high speed films, 142
Underwater Weapons Research Establishment (British), 19, 90, 130
Underworld, 91–93, 123
United Nations (UN), infiltrated, 43–44
United States counterintelligence, *see* Federal Bureau of Investigation
United States intelligence, *see* Central Intelligence Agency
United States military intelligence, 5

Vaginal transmitters, 145–46
Vandenberg Air Force Base (U.S.), 5
Vassall, William John, 19, 56, 88–91
Vera (former swallow), 46–60, 89, 145
 background of, 47–48
 defects, 58
 fears of, 46–47
 first assignment given, 57–58
 KGB agents contact, 48–49
 training of, 49–57
  sexual, 51–56
Verkhonoye House of Love (spy school), 33, 35, 46, 50, 58, 89
Victoria (Queen of England), 150
Video-tapes, *see* Photographic equipment
Vienna Convention on Diplomatic Relations, 74
Vogel, Wolfgang, 59
Volkoff, Konstantin, 114
Volkova, Zinaida Grigorievna, 72–73

Walsingham, Sir Francis, 4

INDEX

Ward, Stephen, 131–34
War Office (British), 4
Watergate scandal, 20
Wendland, Gen. Horst, 111
Wendland, Ilse, 111
Wessel, Gen. Gerhard, 111
Western intelligence agencies
  laxity of, 17
  nickname given Gaczyna by, 37
  reluctant to make use of sexpionage, 20–21
  See also specific Western intelligence agencies
West German counterintelligence, *see* Bundesamt für Verfassungsschutz
West German Federal Intelligence Service, *see* Bundesnachrichtendienst
West German military counterintelligence (Militärischer Abschirmdienst), 102–3, 105
West Germany (Federal Republic of Germany), number of spies in (1966), 115
Wetjen, Johanna, 94
Whitelaw, William, 71
Wigg, George, 74
World War I (1914–1918), 4
World War II (1939–1945), 7, 19, 126–28
Wynne, Greville, 28
Wyszinski, Stefan Cardinal, 85

Yagoda, Henrik, 25
Yezhov, Nikolai, 25–26
Yugoslav intelligence services, 86, 87

Zell air base (West German), 118–21
Zenzen, Alois, 109